BEing *the* Present

101 WAYS TO INSPIRE LIVING AND GIVING

Pilar Stella &
Cynthia Aliza Blake

MORGAN JAMES PUBLISHING • NEW YORK

BEing *the* Present

ISBN: 978-1-60037-515-6 (Paperback)
ISBN: 978-1-60037-516-3 (Hardcover)

Library of Congress Control Number: 2008940012

Published by:

MORGAN · JAMES
THE ENTREPRENEURIAL PUBLISHER ™
www.morganjamespublishing.com

Morgan James Publishing, LLC
1225 Franklin Ave Suite 325
Garden City, NY 11530-1693
Toll Free 800-485-4943
www.MorganJamesPublishing.com

Cover/Interior Design by:
Rachel Lopez
rachel@r2cdesign.com

May this book inspire you
to live and give fully.

Testimonials

There is no greater gift that we can give to ourselves and others than being in the moment. Pilar and Cynthia offer you uplifting and inspiring stories that can help you live your own life with more peace and harmony and find meaning in every moment. This book is a delightful reminder of what is truly important.

~ BARBARA DEANGELIS PH.D. #1 NY TIMES BESTSELLING
AUTHOR, *HOW DID I GET HERE? FINDING YOUR WAY
TO RENEWED HOPE AND HAPPINESS WHEN LIFE
AND LOVE TAKE UNEXPECTED TURNS*

In *BEing the Present*, Pilar & Cynthia are conscious about harmonizing their daily life with their core values. Finally! A book about the journey and importance of creating a sense of "abundance" moment by moment in our families, our communities, our work, and our lives.

~ COLORADO LIEUTENANT GOVERNOR BARBARA O'BRIEN

Pilar and Cynthia are the embodiment of living and giving freely! These two women excel at inspiration, joy and sharing. Get inside their hearts as you read this delightful book.

~ CAROLYN McCORMICK, www.SuccessCoachforLife.com

Life is a series of moments—so living and giving moments should be our daily priority. Life lessons from personal experiences on how to "live" and "give" moments are featured in this simple yet profound book.

~ EMME TOMIMBANG, EMME'S ISLAND MOMENTS, HAWAII TV PERSONALITY

How to Use This Book

We don't live our lives in a linear fashion, and we certainly don't expect everyone to read this book in that way, cover to cover. Have you ever just opened up a book and it happens to fall on a page that has some little nugget of information that fits your life perfectly?

Being present in the moment sometimes means just opening a page of this book and finding exactly what you need—whether it's some snippet of truth from a story or a quote that makes you reflect upon your life. However, if you do want to read the book cover to cover, please do. Here's what you'll notice about how we set the book up for you.

First, while there are themes that run through the book, there's no order to how they are presented. We purposefully chose not to group the book in themes because that seemed to go against its spirit. Also because these represent moments of living and giving, sometimes both of us felt inspired to write on a subject while other times just one of us felt particularly moved to expound on a topic. For the sections we both felt inclined to write, you'll find these pages "split" by the book logo with both of our thoughts. There's no rhyme or reason to why both of us have chimed in on the subject, it just is. That's the beingness of this book!

So please accept the book for what it is as you make your own journey through finding out what "is" for you!

Table of Contents

Foreword

Yesterday is history. Tomorrow is a mystery.
And today? Today is a gift.
That's why we call it the present.

~ BABATUNDE OLATUNJI

We started writing this book to celebrate moments, to practice living in the moment, and to inspire others to live more fully. Little did we know of all the wonderful gifts that would emerge as we journeyed through this process. We found that living in the moment or being present is about giving of ourselves not only to others, but also to ourselves.

We have learned that we all have a purpose. It is in sharing our stories with others, including our weaknesses and strengths as well as our gifts and passions that we may grow and awaken to love and abundance. We are learning that if we choose to live fully, we have more to give, and by giving to ourselves, we may live more fully. This is the gift that is life. Living in the moment is the greatest gift of all.

Living fully to give fully.

~ PILAR STELLA

Nine months before writing this book, I thought about going back to school and getting my Ph.D. I told myself that I needed to get my Ph.D. in order to write a book. Four years earlier, I had wanted to write a book and remember saying to myself, "What have I got to offer the world? I'm only in my early thirties; I better wait until I have more life experience." I kept thinking that at some point down the road that the right time would magically materialize.

> *It's only when we truly know and understand that we have a limited time on earth—and that we have no way of knowing when our time is up—that we will begin to live each day to the fullest, as if it was the only one we had.*

~ ELISABETH KUBLER-ROSS

I was pleasantly surprised to find that all I had to do was just sit down at my computer and start writing. The writing process itself helped me overcome the obstacles in my head. And that is what this book is about—letting go and living in the moment. As I have been riding the wave called life over the past few months of writing this book, this is the first time I have felt emotions that I never even imagined possible. Waves of fear or self-doubt have been washed away by moments of clarity, gratitude, love, self-trust, belief, and faith.

> *You give but little when you give of your possessions. It is when*
> *you give of yourself that you truly give.*
>
> ~ KAHLIL GIBRAN

One of the things that emerged through this process has been the lesson of *giving*. I have learned along this journey that giving is the centerpiece of life—that by giving to myself first, I am able to give so much more to others. Giving is life changing, a multi-dimensional, continuous transformational process. It is why we are here—to give to ourselves and to others.

> *Hold the memory, release the gift.*
> ~ CYNTHIA ALIZA BLAKE

I often find myself straddling the giant canyon that exists between my head and my heart. My thinking-self longs to be rational. It is my ego—the logical part that wants to be able to fit everything neatly in a box so that others can easily understand what I'm trying to say. But I've never fit well into the rules and structures prescribed by society, so my heart-self tells me to move with the energy of what feels right and good. It knows the purity of peace, and I like it there. So, while I'm aware that I straddle these two worlds, I have to remind myself that in every moment we have a choice, and I have to choose what part of me fits in that moment.

Life holds an abundance of joy, love, laughter, and harmony. The question is: are you willing to allow these gifts to flow into your life? If so, when? Are you part of the flow of giving and receiving? Or is the flow stopping at your hands? Getting ready or "waiting until I have this or that," holds us back from ourselves, from our families, and from our world community.

We have begun to shift our consciousness as a planet. This is powerful. I feel the energy of this change daily as I become aware of people and the projects of change that are being birthed and nurtured. My dream of bringing together the force of simple giving on the planet has evolved through the writing of this book. I want to help others become aware of what they're straddling so that they are more at peace with themselves. For only when we are at peace with ourselves can we can help bring peace to the world.

There are always two choices, two paths to take.
One is easy, and that is its only reward.

~ UNKNOWN

OneGiving

~ PILAR STELLA AND CYNTHIA ALIZA BLAKE

Through the process of writing this book together our vision emerged. As we wrote more every day, gratitude and giving overflowed. We did not know where it would take us, but we leapt forward with faith to create *OneGiving*.

Leap, and the net will appear.

~ JOHN BURROUGHS

Our hope is that through this book you will be inspired to live more fully, to appreciate every moment, and to give with grace and gratitude.

We cannot live only for ourselves. A thousand fibers connect us
with our fellow men; and among those fibers,
as sympathetic threads, our actions run as courses,
and they come back to us as effects.

~ HERMAN MELVILLE

Introduction I

To live fully or not to live, that is the quest.
~ PILAR STELLA

The dream was always running ahead of me.
To catch up, to live for a moment in unison with it,
that was the miracle.
~ ANAIS NIN

Growing up I learned that life is hard. I always thought that I must have a plan and work hard to get ahead. Life was never about the journey—it was always about the destination. Life was not about finding or being myself but making sure I did not stop until I arrived. Then once I arrived at a goal, I would immediately move on to identify and reach for the next goal, barely even recognizing that I had achieved my goal and certainly not stopping for a moment to revel in that moment of success. Life was not about opening up my heart and feeling my emotions; it was about doing. Every day, I forgot to stop and smell the flowers along the way. I forgot to breathe. I stopped dreaming.

I found myself "woo busy"—that *whew I'm too busy* feeling—all the time, darting from one thing to the next, in search of whatever "it" was at my destination. I would find that when I did arrive at a goal, the "it" that I was looking for, was never there. So I would go on and set my sights on the next thing, the next achievement, the next goal, the next place to live and so on. I'd be on my way again.

I recognized that this pattern could have gone on forever. Although I always wanted more, I never knew what more was or how to get more.

So my journey began. I read books, sought counseling, but still I did not find "it." I traveled in search of something, though I was not sure what. I looked for jobs here, there, and everywhere, yet I still did not find "it."

I could tell a long story about my journey to find "it" and my frustrations along the way. However, I would rather share my experience from realizing that in searching for more, I was missing the true "it"—what I share with you in this book. My hope is that what I found will inspire you.

> *To live for results would be to sentence myself*
> *to continuous frustration. My only sure reward is*
> *in my actions and not from them.*
> ~ Hugh Prather

In 2007, I was with a group of women at a leadership seminar working toward a goal when a few coaches came in to determine if we had achieved our goal. They assessed our work and began picking apart what we thought we had completed. Not only had we not completed the task, but we certainly were not even doing it "right," which has always been what I was striving for. Back to work we went on our tasks; back in the coaches came to tell us that we still had not completed our task. This happened a few times. No matter how close we thought we got to achieving our goal, we never arrived.

Finally, it hit me! For me, the activity was not really about reaching some unattainable goal, some unattainable "it." It was about living and being in the moment. Not only that, but it was about having fun and living fully along the way.

I realized as a result of this activity that not only did I not know how to live in the moment, but I was not very good at it. I thought, "Well that is silly, how could I be good at something I have never really attempted, lived, or truly experienced?" I realized that this experience was a powerful metaphor for my life!

Rather than beat myself up about the fact that I had not been living in the present and did not really know how to, I thought about what I could do differently. I realized that continuing to do what I was doing was insanity.

Insanity: Doing the same thing over and over again and expecting different results.

~ ALBERT EINSTEIN

I desperately wanted to do something different, yet I could not reconcile the fact that for me, achieving a goal and living in the moment seemed mutually exclusive. That is, having fun and living in the moment did not seem possible to do in the midst of achieving a goal, let alone fulfilling my life's dreams.

So I let go of that thinking and I found three simple principles to guide me:

Trust yourself

Surrender

Live in the moment.

Principle #1

TRUST YOURSELF

Just trust yourself, then you will know how to live.
~ JOHANN WOLFGANG VON GOETHE

Often times in life, I have felt the need to look to others for my answers or to validate me. I have looked to others to figure out who I am and what I want. Other times, I have held back my truths because of my fear of failure, my fear of being rejected or disliked, or my fear of not getting it right. Sometimes I have gone so fast in a million different directions that I have not even heard the little voice within or gotten to know who I am or even know that the answers are within me.

Every time you don't follow your inner guidance, you feel a loss of energy, a loss of power, a sense of spiritual deadness.
~ SHAKTI GAWAIN

Trusting yourself is about spending some time getting to know yourself. Look at any of your self-doubts, your desire to be like others or to be liked by others, and trust yourself to have the right answers for you within. What is right for others isn't necessarily what is right for you. When you begin to hear negative self-talk, negativity, or self-doubt, remember to trust yourself. Listen to your gut and trust your instinct.

> *Be what you are. This is the first step*
> *toward becoming better than you are.*
>
> ~ JULIUS CHARLES HARE

Trust yourself to look within because the answers will always come. When they do come, follow them and trust them. Always remember that by trusting yourself you will find out who you really are and all that you can be.

> *All my life I had been looking for something, and*
> *everywhere I turned someone tried to tell me what it was.*
> *I accepted their answers too, though they were often in*
> *contradiction and even self-contradictory. I was naïve. I was*
> *looking for myself and asking everyone except myself questions*
> *which I, and only I, could answer. It took me a long time and*
> *much painful boomeranging of my expectations to achieve a*
> *realization everyone else appears to have been born with:*
> *that I am nobody but myself.*
>
> ~ RALPH ELLISON

Principle #2
SURRENDER

In the end what matters most is
How well did you live
How well did you love
How well did you learn to let go.

~ BUDDHIST PROVERB

Many people have a hard time with this word. They think surrender means quitting or giving up. For me, it means letting go—letting go of my expectations of how something should look or be and enjoying what is. Surrender means making the choice not to get pulled down by negative energy, walking away from what is not working, and shifting into and being the source of positive energy, inspiration compassion, and empathy.

When something is frustrating you or someone is bothering you, things do not look how you would like them to look. But when things are not working for you, that is the time when you need to breathe deep, relax, and surrender to what is. You have the option to stay in a negative state of mind or to let go. Only you can make that choice—to accept what is, move on, and create what you want in your life.

The most difficult lesson to learn is
which bridge in life to use or which one to break off.

~ UNKNOWN

Principle #3

LIVE IN THE MOMENT

We do not remember days,
We remember moments.

~ CESARE PAVESE

For some, living in the moment is a foreign concept. We are impatient. We scurry from task to task, thinking "Wow! Look at how much I have accomplished in my life," only to realize at some point that our lives have just passed us by.

I was one of those people. Living in the moment always seemed impossible. Though I had lived much of my life with this mindset, I no longer wanted to live this way. For me, letting my life pass me by was not an option. I had a sense of urgency to turn it around sooner rather than later.

I don't want to get to the end of my life
and find that I lived just the length of it.
I want to have lived the width of it as well.

~ DIANE ACKERMAN

Despite my desire to live fully, I realized that I was not very good at living in the moment. How could I be? The concept was brand new to me. It would be like expecting a baby who takes his or her first steps to start running immediately after those same first steps.

For so long, I could not reconcile between living in the moment and achieving my dreams and goals. If I was not very good, effective, or efficient at living in the moment, then surely I could not complete or achieve any let alone all of the dreams and goals in my heart. I could not reconcile the seriousness of completing a task or achieving a goal with my perception of the frivolity of living in the moment.

> *To change one's life: Start immediately.*
> *Do it flamboyantly. No exceptions.*
> ~ WILLIAM JAMES

That is when I decided to write this book. I did it not only to help others learn how to take baby steps toward living in the moment, but to give myself some guidance in learning how to live in the moment as well. I have big dreams, but as I take these small steps, I find that I'm better able to reach and to strive for those dreams. I am learning that if I choose to live fully, I have more to give, and by giving to myself and others, I may live more fully.

Introduction II

Living with love and abundance.
~ CYNTHIA ALIZA BLAKE

Life in abundance comes only through great love.
~ ELBERT HUBBARD

My life has been and continues to be an abundant experience. Growing up in the American South during the '60s, I experienced extremes—from the safety of a loving home to the fear brought on by racial hatred and physical abuse. But, I see it *all* as a gift that continues to inspire me today.

For many years, I had no idea what a blessing my childhood experiences were. It took me a long time to fully understand that we can learn goodness and peace in the hard experiences of life. I'm not sure we ever truly know the gift of our experiences when they are happening, but I do know that now, in hindsight, I have learned.

I was blessed to spend my early childhood with my grandmother, a woman of incredible wisdom and beauty. She was a channeled healer, constantly in touch with the divine. To me, she was simply the softest and most loving memory of my youth. I spent the first eight years of my life enjoying my grandparent's expansive family farm. It was a working farm for my grandparents. For me it was a playground unlike any I would ever experience again complete with seemingly endless pastures full of all kinds of mammal friends. There were two lakes filled with fish and orchards full of succulent fruit. I swear my grandmother—whom I called Mammy— had the biggest watermelon and cantaloupe patch ever. The chicken houses were overflowing with chickens, ducks, and my favorite, the ginnies. My job was to find the ginny-hen eggs. They were a secretive bird, and you had to follow them very carefully to find their nests. If they thought they were being spied upon, they wouldn't go back! It was wonderful and adventurous, and it was filled with love and bliss for life. I didn't know how wonderful it was until it was gone, and it took me many years to find the same love and peace of my childhood.

After my grandmother's passing, I went to live with my parents in a notably poor neighborhood in Louisiana. They were unfamiliar to me, and it took me a long time to really get to know my parents. They were from different sides of the track, but I came to understand their blending as a powerful experience for me. In my home, I learned the many faces of love and pain. My inside world was as turbulent and violent as the outside world. Racial riots occurred without warning; often my school would be closed without warning. There were a lot of angry people shooting guns. Death was everywhere, and it was ugly and scary. I often felt alone, spending most of my time dreaming of faraway places and a fairy-tale life. Like my beloved ginny hens, I had to carve the right hiding place that no one would find so that those things I held close wouldn't be taken away. With my heart closed as protection, I learned how to "survive" as situations presented themselves.

Many years passed. As I woke from a near-death experience after hemorrhaging severely during the emergency cesarean-section of my son, the message was clear: I have a purpose. As I held my son, I realized that I had a choice. I could continue to live my life closed-off and afraid, or I could choose to do something different. I could begin to find the love I had as a young child.

When my little one was a year old, my father died of cancer. I had been afraid of him for so long, but as he lay on his death-bed, he told me something that has shaped who I am today. He said, "There's only one thing to know about life. If you don't like how something is, you're the only one who as the ability to change you."

During this same time, I was diagnosed with a life-threatening condition. This was during the early 1980s, and I had two doctors tell me that I didn't have much of a chance. Remembering what my father had said, I went to a third doctor who told me "If you change your diet and lifestyle, it's *possible* that you could have a positive effect on your disease." I took the "what's possible" option, and it was then that everything fell into place. I took ownership of my body and that made it possible to take ownership of what goes on inside of me, in my *heart*. That's what opened me back to love and the possibility of what comes with love—abundance, a fulfillment, a fullness of one's self, one's being.

It is in sharing our gifts and passions that we may awaken to live with love and abundance. I am filled with gratitude for my life and for the people that have touched my life. I hope that with this book I can help waken the love and abundance that lies within you.

101 Ways to Inspire Living and Giving

We are invited to put aside our wish list, our goals, and be open to experiencing our life fully in each moment, listening to each moment, responding to each moment.

~ BARBARA DeANGELIS

1. Give.

The wise man does not lay up his treasures.
The more he gives to others,
the more he has for his own.

~ Lao Tsu

Just because you are seventy is no excuse to give up and let
others make your decisions for you. The fact that you are still
alive is reason enough to believe that you are here for a purpose;
and that purpose is to learn, to teach, and to give.

~ Thomas D. Willhite

It is in giving that we feel connected. I was always taught by my father to be very generous. My father was always giving, even when we did not have very much. He definitely taught me to be generous and giving. When we would go out to dinner, he would always offer to pay for everyone—he always got the bill. In fact, we still joke about how it's not okay to mess with my Italian father when it comes to paying the bill. I learned from him that what "comes around goes around," and that you get so much in return when you give.

3

There are many ways to give. Often times when people think of giving, they immediately think of money. Yet, there are so many different ways to give, including giving one's self, giving time, giving resources, giving support, giving skills, giving love, as well as giving money.

Despite being taught generosity, I found that I have always been very giving in every way except to myself. In fact, I am often giving to a fault, meaning that I give and give and give to others and when my gas tank runs on empty, I forget to fill up for myself.

This past year, I started to really give to myself. Although it was weird and uncomfortable at first, I realized that when I allowed myself to give to me first, then I could give to others. Once I started giving to myself, I realized that I could also give more to others. The funny thing is that as I have begun to give more to organizations that I care about and causes that I am passionate about, I am beginning to see that more opportunities are flying my way.

I have heard people say that when I have more, I will give more. While they usually are talking about money, it doesn't matter. My advice is, don't wait! Seriously, even if it is a little bit, *give*. Because it is in giving that we are ONE. In giving, we can change the world and make a difference.

We receive when we give. Giving comes in many forms. Most of us think giving is about money. Giving is an energy, just like money is energy. The power of giving comes from the intention behind the giving. When we give of ourselves in service, if it is from our essence, our beingness, it is from a place of love. The world is full of givers, and if our intention is to give from a place of love, then we expand as beings. It is our choice to see the world as giving.

I learned this from my grandmother. Everything on my grandparent's farm was bartered and they shared everything they had. My grandmother, Mammy, was often called on to help the sick and the dying. She was the one who prepared the bodies of people when they had passed on. But no matter what she faced, her house was a warm and inviting place for the entire community.

She chose to give of herself in every situation, so from her I learned that unconditional love is pure giving. Life was simple; living in the moment was natural and easy. Mammy always had time to tell me stories, teach me to roll dough, make pies and jam. She was always happy and because of her example, I know that when you love without condition, the flow of giving happens easily and with joy.

Giving is powerful when it comes from love. Give when you are ready—when you feel it. As we each shift into a place of giving, we will heal ourselves, each other, and our planet.

2. Be open to receiving.

The flow of giving and receiving is much simpler than we often allow it to be. The giving part has always been easier for me to accept than the receiving part because I grew up hearing the message "it's better to give than to receive." My question is…says who? And better than what?

Okay, I have spent many years of my life thinking and living with this question. I began to ponder this idea of giving and receiving for the first time as I traveled around the world. I found that in the yin and yang of all things there is balance. Just as night follows day, just as there is male and female, there is giving and receiving.

The power of grasping, of really getting this concept is life altering and is the key to both giving and receiving. Being open to receiving all that we are meant to receive is what happens when we align with and are connected to God, Buddha, Jesus, Krishna, or what ever name you choose to call your divine source.

In order to receive we must believe we are worthy of receiving. Wanting something, regardless of what it is—money, a partner, a job—is a great place, even a necessary place, to start the receiving process. It is true that "giving starts the receiving process," but we must be open to receiving that which we have asked for. Being open is the worthiness of receiving, and believing in one's self is the doorway to being open to receiving all that you are meant to receive.

Late one cold winter evening, my friend offered to take me home. When we were on our way, she turned to me and said, "Thank you for letting me drive you home." I looked at her a bit puzzled and asked, "What do you mean, shouldn't I be thanking you?" She said she was really glad to get the opportunity to support me because I was always supporting others and often did not give others the opportunity to give to me. Wow, what a realization that was for me.

How often do I go through my life giving so much to others, not giving to myself, and not being open to receiving? Here was my chance and not only did it feel good for me, it felt good for my friend too! What a gift she gave me—not just the one of driving me home, but the gift of allowing myself to be open to receiving. The next time you get a chance to receive, take it in and fully appreciate it!

3 . Be grateful.

Gratitude unlocks the fullness of life.
It turns what we have into enough, and more.
It turns denial into acceptance, chaos to order, confusion to
clarity. It can turn a meal into a feast, a house into a home, a
stranger into a friend. Gratitude makes sense of our past, brings
peace for today, and creates a vision for tomorrow.
~ Melody Beattie

I have not always been grateful. I grew up saying "grace," before meals and prayers before bed. They were all prayers of gratitude, but in reality, I merely recited the words, never really feeling what they were all about. Since then, my life has become filled with moments of gratitude.

I remember the day I became aware of the beauty of gratitude. I was attending a yoga conference in San Francisco. One of the gurus told us about a restaurant that vibrated gratitude in everything they served. This I had to experience.

"Cafe Gratitude" was an awakening for me. It is a vegan eating establishment complete with menu items like: "I am giving," "I am loving," "I am passionate," "I am abundant." Wow! The water is served in containers that have inspirational words on them like "peace," "love," or "joy." The servers are all happy to be of service. When your food is served, it is joyfully placed in front of you with the words, "You are giving." "You are loving." "You are passionate," depending on what you have ordered. As I enjoyed this amazing live food with friends, I felt my being shift into a place I never realized existed. I felt light, love, joy and gratitude. I bought the game and workbook the owners of Cafe Gratitude created, took it home, devoured it, shared it and began to live it.

Each day before I get out of bed, I bring to mind all that I am grateful for. I also keep a gratitude journal filled with actions and experiences in my day that I am truly thankful for, and I absolutely know that all that is beautiful comes from this attitude of gratitude in my life.

Of all the "attitudes" we can acquire,
surely the attitude of gratitude is the most important
and by far the most life-changing.
~ Zig Ziglar

Because of all that I experienced as a teen and young adult, I often focused on the negative and didn't recognize the positive in my life. Isn't this how so many of us are raised? We have been raised in a consciousness in which the media, people, and society focus on what isn't going well rather than what is. In other words, we live in a victim consciousness.

What if every day each of us began to only focus on what was going right in our day, our life, and our world? In order for things to go right in our lives, we have to appreciate all that is. When we do that, we can begin to experience a shift from the negative toward a gratitude consciousness. This is powerful. If we not only look for the positive but are grateful for it, this lifts our vibrational state to a very high place. This increases the flow of whatever it is that we want into our lives.

It's a beautiful, upward cycle. Increase the flow of positive energy, the energy of abundance, by increasing your gratitude for all that is, and you'll find that the more you're grateful for what is good, the more good you will get.

When I begin to focus on what I am grateful for, the other bad things melt away. The more grateful I am every day, the better my day becomes. What are you grateful for?

4. Dare to dream.

There are some people who live in a dream world,
and there are some who face reality; and then
there are those who turn one into the other.
~ Douglas Everett

The first time I saw this quote it resonated with me. I was often told as a child to stop dreaming and to get my head out of the clouds. I was trained to think only in terms of what is realistic, pragmatic, and responsible. Yet a part of me was dying inside—the part that believed, the part that had fun, and the part that dreamed.

When I read Everett's quote, I knew that I had begun to dream again, and more important, that there was nothing wrong with dreaming. In fact, I finally started to believe that by dreaming, I could achieve things and live fully. For you see, dreaming creates a future, so without dreaming, what is the point of living? So here I am writing, creating, believing and finally dreaming—ready to turn my dreams into reality. Now that is what life is all about!

You may say I'm a dreamer, but I'm not the only one…
I hope someday you will join us, and
the world will live as one.

~ JOHN LENNON

Dreams are the window from which I leap. As a child I was the dreamer, often finding myself being pulled back from a daydream in the middle of class. I could sit for hours, dreaming of far away places, of beautiful dresses, and of the perfect husband and family.

I still dream, but now my dreams are intentional. I consciously create my "now" when I dream. Today my dreams are less like a fairytale and more true to who I want to be and what I want to create in my life. It's an amazing experience to dream and have it arrive, often just the way I envisioned it to be, and sometimes even bigger.

Be childlike—dream big, wild, amazing dreams. Believe it is possible, feel it in your being, and live your dreams.

5. TRAVEL.

When I travel I have no idea what's in store for me,
but if I'm wise
and understand the art of travel,
I let myself go into the stream of the unknown
and accept whatever comes in the spirit.

~ FREYA STARK

The moment that the wheels of any plane I'm on leave the tarmac, I am transported into a new dimension. The comfort of home and the security of what is familiar grows smaller and smaller as I look out the tiny window and see the land disappear. The hum of the jet engine puts my mind into a meditation as I become grateful for where I have been and excited for the journey ahead.

I have traveled often—from the jetting mountains of Nepal, the rolling vineyards in France, and the bustling streets of Mexico to the expansive stretches of beaches in Indonesia. It is the source of my creativity and inspiration. Travel opens the door to experiences that take me out of the familiar and awakens my connection with humankind.

The first time I voyaged outside the comfort of America, I flew for eighteen hours and landed in a most unfamiliar region,

Papua New Guinea. As the jet approached the runway, my heart beat with excitement, and I felt great warmth in my soul. As I looked outside the window, the runway was lined with children waiving at our airplane. How amazing! It was dark outside; morning was still an hour away. Yet the entire village was there to welcome our arrival; I could see their silhouettes in the early morning dark.

As I walked down the steps of the aircraft, I felt a surge of excitement and inhaled the sweet, intoxicating aroma of cloves. I had arrived in one of the most treasured places on the planet. Greeted by dancers, chiefs in head-dress, men, children, and women with their babies bundled in their arms, I felt welcomed— more so than at any other destination that I had ever been in my life. The sun rose with a glowing radiance that captured my breath then, as it does now, remembering that feeling of welcome. I had traveled thousands of miles from New York to be greeted with love, kindness, and open arms.

From this first experience and throughout my other travels, I have consistently found that the vulnerability of allowing myself to being a stranger in a different land has helped me to feel a deep and strong connection to humankind and the planet.

Traveling is a way of seeing our own lives and the lives of others from a new perspective. By traveling, meeting people who are different from ourselves, and immersing ourselves in different cultures and customs, we may begin to appreciate our own lives, homes, families, communities—all the things in our lives. New journeys allow us to see that although many customs, cultures, and lifestyles are very different from our own, we as people are actually more similar than different.

By getting this perspective, we can appreciate our own lives and also have more respect for other people's ways of being. Whenever possible, get out and travel. Take the opportunity to get a fresh perspective on your own life, appreciate the lives of others, and find a connection to our greater humanity.

6. Do not be afraid to fail.

*Only those who dare to fail greatly
can ever achieve greatly.*
~ John F. Kennedy

As a little girl, failure never seemed like an option. I was protected from everything and was discouraged from taking risks. Everything was about being careful and not letting bad things happen. As I got older, life continued to be very safe, "perfect," very controlled, and very unfulfilling.

As I reached out to attempt new things, I was uncomfortable and afraid. This concept of taking risks no matter what—even if I failed—was totally new to me. I have to say that I still don't like to fail, yet I am beginning to realize that with each failure, there is a tremendous opportunity to learn and grow. Now I can see that from the greatest failures come some of the greatest gifts. I am just beginning to realize that living life now and living life fully means going out there and doing things that make me happy, doing things that feel good, and not being afraid to mess up. When I trust that I am doing what is meant to be, what is right for me, then I don't fear failing. That's a wonderful place to be.

We fear failing from our birth. Think about it. As we emerge from the comfort of the womb, we are thrust into a potentially dangerous world. Some of us use this fear to keep from finding our passion, our gifts, and our dreams.

I remember when I was growing up, one of my favorite things was to jump out of the barn into a pile of leaves. I jumped trusting that the leaves would offer me safety, a cushion from my fall. I'm certain the ground was hard; however, I have no memory of it being hard, nor did I ever get hurt from jumping over and over again.

The leaves represent our inner knowing. When I jumped, I knew that I wouldn't get hurt. In other words, I trusted myself. The more we trust that inner knowing, the more we're able to risk—to reach out—without fear.

The memory of succeeding, of jumping out that barn door over and over, serves as an important reminder. Everyday, there are opportunities to take a risk, from saying something we feel is important to reaching out to help a stranger, from dreaming something big and deciding to do it, to dancing wildly because it feels good.

Look for reasons to go for it, and have fun in the process. After all, what's the worse thing that could happen? What's the best outcome imaginable? Reaching for our dreams is easier when we reflect on our past successes and trust our inner-knowingness.

7. GIVE AN ANONYMOUS GIFT.

Your giving is sacred and therefore
should be kept secret. It is wise to give
quietly with no strings attached...
~ CATHERINE PONDER

Giving an anonymous gift is so much fun! Whether it is something small like buying coffee for the people in line behind you, paying a toll booth for someone random, or something bigger like volunteering your time at a local homeless shelter, there is nothing like the feeling of satisfaction you get when you give.

I had a friend who recently told a story about one of his excursions to dinner with his wife in which they gave an anonymous gift. He related that as they were eating dinner, a group of teenagers came in for a post-prom dinner. He and his wife thought how fun it would be to buy them all dinner. So they paid for the kids' dinner and told the waiter to keep their gift anonymous. They sat and watched the whole thing and said there was nothing like the excitement, delight, and complete disbelief on some of the kids' faces at the fact that someone would do something so thoughtful and random.

The next time you get a chance to give an anonymous gift, go ahead and revel in the recipient's delight! It truly is an opportunity to practice giving on a whole new level.

8. Do something different.

Changing things up a little in your life and adding a little diversity will help you to appreciate what you have. Doing something different may help you find ways to appreciate new or different ways of doing things. You may even learn that the new ways are better than your old ways.

Change may be as insignificant as as getting out of bed a different way, sleeping on a different side of the bed, or turning the role of toilet paper around. It may include walking, riding a bike, or taking a bus to work instead of driving. It may be switching your schedule around, going out instead of staying in, or trying out activities that you never would have done before.

Whatever the change may be, try it out and see how much your life can change for the better when you shake things up a little. Do something different for 101 days and see how much more fun you have, how much easier it is to adapt to change, and how much more comfortable you become with change.

9. Take a minute to stop and look around.

Life moves pretty fast. If you don't stop to look around once in a while you could miss it.

~ From the movie *Ferris Bueller's Day Off*

I love rainbows. I am so amazed at the absolute splendor, magnificence, and perfection of rainbows. When I was a little girl, they seldom occurred, yet when they did, it was as though I was under their spell. I also wanted to find the pot of gold that everyone promised lay at its end. Whenever a rainbow appeared, I would run in the direction of its end—but the end always eluded me.

For me, a rainbow is an invitation to look. It is my trigger that creates an opportunity to pause. And when I look, this is what I find: everything always looks brighter when there is a rainbow. Like magic, it appears in the sky and then disappears without warning. While it is there, I feel the magnificence of life. I feel I can achieve the impossible, that all my dreams can come true.

I invite you to find your trigger, the thing that prompts you to stop and look around at the absolute splendor and perfection of creation. I'm older now, yet in my child's eye, I have come to realize the pot of gold is me and my ability to stop and marvel. Find your moment of awe so that you too can discover your miracle of absolute perfection.

10. Look directly into people's eyes.

*When there is love in the heart
there are rainbows in the eyes, which cover
every black cloud with gorgeous hues.*
~ Henry Ward Beecher

*I need no dictionary of quotations to remind me
that the eyes are the windows of the soul.*
~ Max Beerbohm

We see in others what we also see in ourselves. When we look into the eyes of another, we connect. There in the eyes of another we see love and pain, hope and sadness, joy and laughter. Strangers become friends. And if we allow ourselves to feel, we can also see ourselves.

In the eyes of others we see ourselves, realizing we are all connected. We see the beauty of another and the reflection of ourselves in another.

Start by looking, really looking into the eyes of someone you love or care for deeply. I'm sure emotion wells-up inside of you when you do this. Now look into the eyes of a stranger with the same emotion as you did your loved-one, and you may find the same beauty and love looking back at you. If we allow ourselves this gift, soon we all become brothers and sisters.

11. BE OF SERVICE.

It is in the giving of ourselves that we truly experience gratitude. Community is the connection we feel for humankind. So many times we focus on all the things we do not have and get fixated on the negative. Spending time with others and giving back to the community helps take us outside of ourselves and our lives. Being of service and giving back allows us to put our lives in perspective and oftentimes see how much we really have. It allows us to be grateful for everything we have.

Giving to others can help us focus on all that is going well in our lives rather than all that is wrong. It can allow us to see all that we have rather than all the things we do not have. The next time you get caught up in the negative, get out and be of service.

12. Turn a negative into a positive.

No pessimism ever discovered the secrets of the stars,
or sailed to an unchartered land, or
opened a new heaven to the human spirit.

~ Helen Keller

Every time something negative happens to us, we have an opportunity. We can choose to have the incident set us back, or we can learn from it, heal, and move forward in our lives.

Here's an extreme example: say one country bombs another country. The country that was bombed doesn't retaliate by bombing; instead, it builds a school or a hospital in the country that bombed it. This does happen, but imagine what would happen if something like this happened every time a bomb was dropped?

The next time you do something negative or something negative happens to you, look for the opportunity within and turn it around to find at least one positive thing that you can do to counteract the negative. Turn your frown into a smile. If someone comes at you with anger, acknowledge them and return

31

their anger with admiration. There are infinite ways to do this; you're only limited by your creativity.

If you try this over and over again, at some point it will become routine, and you will find a positive opportunity in every experience.

13. DRIVE THE SPEED LIMIT.

I tend to speed through every aspect of my life, and my driving is definitely a metaphor for this.

I find that when I am whizzing by cars my driving is often reflective of how I am living my life. But something happens when I drive—and live—this way. When I am in a hurry driving, I miss everything that goes by, and I get impatient and irritable. I worry about what the other drivers are or aren't doing. I get caught up in getting to my destination rather than enjoying the ride. In short, I don't live in the now.

The days that I slow down and actually drive the speed limit are good days! Seriously, I find that when I slow down, I am actually living in the present moment. I am not in a hurry to get to my destination. I am not caught up in the bustle of life; rather I'm enjoying the moments that life has to offer. I actually notice what people are doing in their cars and often get a chuckle at what I see. I spot buildings, signs, or other random events that I never notice when I am in a hurry. The minute I recognize this, it also reminds me to slow down in my life.

And no surprise—the days that I drive the speed limit, I slow down everywhere. I talk to more people, take a minute for myself to breathe and just relax a little. I let go and have more fun.

The next time you find yourself hitting the accelerator, ask yourself "is this how I live my life?" And if it is, perhaps it is time for you to drive the speed limit. At least try it today and see what happens.

14. FACE ADVERSITY.

Every adversity, every failure,
every heartache carries with it the seed
of an equal or greater benefit.
~ NAPOLEON HILL

From the Great Depression to the world wars to the Civil Rights Movement, the generations before mine have had to endure much more loss and overcome greater adversity. On the other hand, we are a generation of perfectionism not endurance. We are a generation of complacency and consumerism, of getting what we want *now*! We are a generation that is much less able to deal with suffering and the unexpected. We are less able to endure and overcome adversity than those before us. So what can we learn from this?

What I am learning is that the result of not being able to face adversity is that I am less able to deal with imperfections. I expect the best, and I expect things to go my way. I come from a generation that has been spoiled, that expects everything to go the way we want—or at least just work out. For me, when things don't go my way, when I fail, when I hit an obstacle or am thrown off guard, my reaction is often to just sit-down, give in, or even worse, give up.

I am fortunate enough to know now that this doesn't always work out well. I am beginning to recognize that by not allowing myself to fail and by avoiding adversity, I am avoiding my life, my dreams, and my passions.

I am beginning to realize that if I really want to make a difference, I have to risk, go for it, and face adversity no matter what the outcome. And if I fail, I can learn from it. Yet if I don't go for it and risk, then I will never know if it is possible.

The next time you come face to face with adversity, look it in the eye, and listen to your intuition to guide you through it because you never know what you will accomplish if you don't take a chance.

15. LISTEN WITH YOUR FULL ATTENTION.

Listening with your full attention is not always the easiest thing to do. Rather, we often get caught up in listening to others from the perspective of "do I agree with what they are saying," "am I right," or "are they wrong?" Sometimes we don't even realize we are doing that. We listen to people to justify or validate our own way of thinking rather than just listening to hear what they are saying, feeling, or experiencing.

Listening with your full attention means really listening and being with that person. It means not walking away from that person and yelling back, "I'm listening honey, keep going." It means not picking up the phone in the middle of a conversation. It means being there and really being willing to hear that person. We are not necessarily accustomed to that and for some of us it may be really difficult to listen in this way.

Really listen! You might just be amazed at what your really hear.

16. DO SOMETHING SPONTANEOUS.

All growth is a leap in the dark, a spontaneous,
unpremeditated act without benefit of experience.
~ HENRY MILLER

It is funny. As I think about this, I realize that I alternate between planning everything or being totally spontaneous. While it is important to plan and think things through, I find that if I do it too much, it keeps me really stuck in my head. Rather, when I do something spontaneous and last minute, I feel completely alive and invariably have a blast.

Whether it is taking off a random day from work when you really need it, flying out of town, or doing something else random and unplanned, it doesn't really matter. Just once in a while, do something fun and spontaneous to give you a little reminder of what life is all about. Life is about living, so get out there and live with gusto!

17. Say no once in a while.

I have found over and over again that I don't know how to say no. I really enjoy spending time with other people and love what that time brings. Yet I have found that sometimes saying yes to others means saying no to myself. In order for me to be able to support myself and those around me, sometimes it requires me saying no to others, setting my boundaries, and prioritizing myself.

For a long time, I found it difficult to say no to others because I feared what they might think or that I might hurt their feelings. But I realized that saying no once in a while is a gift to myself so that I may then be able to give more to others.

I am a pencil in the hand of God.
~ Mother Teresa

The greatest gift I give myself is the power of focus toward my purpose. I spent much of my life getting excited about everything that came my way. Some people call this distraction. It could be called, Jill of all trades, master of none. The reality of focus

41

comes from asking myself three questions when facing options: is this going to enhance my business or life to impact more people? Is taking the time to do something contributing toward my business or play? And what is my priority around making the decision; is it an investment in my business or purpose, or is it play?

If I say yes to everything, it fractures me, and there is no expansion in fractures. By saying no sometimes, by limiting my choices, I get to concentrate on those areas that are important. Often saying *no* is the gift we give ourselves because it provides the freedom to expand those important areas. That is living in joy!

18. Breathe.

Breathe in experience.
~ Muriel Rukeyser

Breath, or Prana, is our physical connection to life. When we are born we take that first breath and begin a journey that by our choice can be anything we dream it to be. Our passage out of this life is our last breath. In-between lies an abundance of breaths connecting us to our source if we are willing to listen.

How can life itself be controlled by a complete involuntary response? Yet when we voluntarily call upon our breath, we have the ability to increase our human potential. Our energy increases as does our health. For an athlete, his or her breath is an integral part of the performance. The breathing process is rapid but controlled as it feeds the physical body and sustains its performance.

Try taking three deep, cleansing breaths next time you get into your car, stop at a red light, turn on the TV, or get out of bed. Calling on our breath is awesome. When that scared feeling arises, just try it and feel light.

43

19. THINK OF WATER.

Nothing is softer or more flexible than water,
yet nothing can resist it.

~ LAO TSU

Water is magical. Water is spiritual. When I think of water, I am instantly transformed to peace and tranquility. There is something mystifying and healing about water. Whether it is the sound of waves crashing on the beach or water flowing from a waterfall, water is calming, soothing, transformational.

My best memories in life are moments when I am near water—swimming, floating, splashing, having fun in the water or just walking along the water's edge. When I get fired up, passionate, worked up, overly agitated or angry, I visualize or think about water and the tension melts away. When I go to water, it soothes and rejuvenates me so I can get back to what I was doing with more peace and serenity. The next time you get overwhelmed or worked up, either go to water or think about water and see if it calms you too.

20. Play a game.

Don't play games, play a game. What I mean is don't play games in life, but once in a while stop and play a game. Whether it is a board game, cards, or some other fun game like hide-and-go-seek, go ahead and have some fun. Why not, what have you got to lose?

We have gotten to be so competitive in this society that we sometime even play games the way we live our lives—we have to win no matter what. I stopped playing games a long time ago because I always felt people were just playing to win. It wasn't about playing the game and having fun.

Recently that changed for me. I started having game nights and getting fun people together to play games just to have fun! Playing games has since become about spending time with people I care about. Now, playing games is about being in the moment, just kicking around, relaxing a little, laughing a lot, and being free from being so serious all the time. The next time you get too serious, call a couple of friends, make some root-beer floats, kick back and play some games.

21. Dance.

We're fools whether we dance or not,
so we might as well dance.

~ Japanese Proverb

When I was little I used to dance, twirl, and swirl around. In my early teens, I'd go to Bar- and Bat-Mitzvahs and break dance. As a teenager, I lived in Italy, and I often went to the Euro-discothèques with my friends. I felt invincible. In college, I danced until dawn—shaking it, salsa-ing, disco-ing, hip hopping, and techno-ing the night away. I had so much fun never worrying about what people thought and just feeling the rhythm. In graduate school, the dancing became tamer and the times I went were fewer and farther between. Then sometime in my mid-twenties, I stopped dancing completely.

One day, I went to a workshop that reminded me of how much I love to dance. I began to throw *Shake Your Booty* parties and remembered what a blast dancing can be! I realized that it got me in touch with my heart and my soul. Now, whenever I'm stuck in my head, am in a bad mood, or just a little frustrated with life, I turn on some fun dance music and bump my booty, shake my rump, and get down. Dancing reminds me to have fun; it replenishes my soul.

Next time someone asks you to dance, don't turn them down or worry that you aren't a good dancer. Just get out there, loosen up, and enjoy the moment. Really, just bounce to the beat, let go, and have fun!

22. THANK OTHERS.

I am so grateful for all the people who have touched my life. Yet I often think to myself, "Have I thanked them lately?" Growing up was not always easy. I was raised in a loving family, but through most of my childhood we were only a family of three: my father, my brother, and me. For a little girl, it was sometimes hard not having a mother around. Yet I was always blessed with amazing and special people in my life. Many of my friends would tell me I must have an angel looking over me. I believe I did have angels watching over me and still do.

We all have angels, yet do we take the time to thank them? How often do we take the time to thank the people in our life who make a difference for us? What if we lived in a world in which we thanked people regularly for who they are and all they do for us? Imagine all of the special moments we could have if we were to thank those people more often.

As I begin to live a life of not holding back, of living fully and being in the moment, I am finding that I am thankful for a lot. Because I am less caught up in the past or the future, I can truly appreciate those people in my life and the world around me who make a difference.

Who have you thanked today?

23. Dive in.

*The surest hindrance of success is to have too high a standard
of refinement in our own minds, or too high an opinion of the
public. He who is determined not to be satisfied with anything
short of perfection will never do anything.*

~ WILLIAM HAZLITT

I remember the first time I stood on a diving board—my legs trembling, my heart pounding in my chest. The water looked so far away. The fact that I was scared of water did not help. My fear of water arose from a near-drowning I experienced in the ocean.

Standing on the edge of the diving board was so scary. I could hear people yelling for me to dive in; the sound of my heart intensified with such strength that it was the only sound I heard. And then as if someone lifted me up and moved my body off the board, I dove in. Wow! That felt awesome—totally liberating and fun!

Reflecting on my diving experience, I have come to realize how easy it can be to create such drama around doing anything. We continually tell ourselves stories that are full of misperceptions and illusions because they're based on someone else's rules and standards. It keeps us on the edge of the proverbial diving board, but we hold ourselves back from realizing our full potential because we're paralyzed by FEAR, "False Events Appearing Real."

Fear of diving off is so limiting and even selfish. When we're at the edge, we get a glimpse of what is possible, yet we still resist jumping in—even when we have something like water to catch us. We make our own fears insurmountable, but how easy and freeing the action is once we decide to just dive in. It sheds the barriers and expectations we have of ourselves.

Rather than worrying about getting things right or perfect, just dive in and get started. So many times I have stopped myself before I even got started because I was worried about the end product; I was worried about getting it right, or I made it out to be too big. What I am realizing is that if I just get started and take the first bite, the second bite doesn't seem so big. And if I am consistent, persistent, disciplined, and focused in taking a little bite every day, the end goal doesn't seem so overwhelming and unmanageable. So, dive in. It is allowing life!

24. Have fun!

A little of what you fancy does you good.
~ Marie Lloyd

Growing up, it felt like everything in my life had to have a purpose. I was taught to get things done, to have goals, to get a lot accomplished. The messages around me were all about how well I was doing in school and which of the best colleges I would go to so that I could graduate and have the most successful job. Of course the goal was to make a lot of money and so I could have a lot of things. Yet, where was the fun in all of that?

The times in my life I associate with the most fun are the moments when I was away from this mentality. When I lived in Italy, life was about enjoying the moment, appreciating the good things in life–food, friends, art, and culture. There, I got to ski for the first time, speak a different language, and meet people from around the world. Now that's my idea of fun.

In college, I had another opportunity to have fun. I went to the University of Wisconsin in Madison, which is often labeled one of the best party schools. So yes, needless to say, I had fun. And the fun wasn't just about partying; it was because I was experiencing life fully, going dancing, and trying new and different things.

Now I live in Colorado, and I continue to find new ways to have fun. It's like one giant playground. In one weekend, I can ski in the mountains one day and ride my bike around Denver the next. How much fun is that?

As I write this, I realize that the times that I have had the most fun in life don't really have to do with the places that I had fun. Rather, it was about the *moments* of fun themselves. The best moments in my life are those when I let go of having to get "it" done and just have fun! And mind you, I have found that I am even able to get things done when I am having fun; in fact, often times I get more done! So get out there and have a little fun. You might even find you get a lot done when you do so, and if not, no worries. Just give yourself a break and have a good time!

25. Love fully.

Love is a choice. In every moment by moment, we are either giving or receiving. When we hold on to love and don't give it away, it will fade into the night, leaving us bewildered and shrouded in doubt. Love!

~ Byron Tuck

*When we come to the last moment of this lifetime,
and we look back across it the only thing
that's going to matter is,
"What was the quality of our love?"*

~ Richard Bach

I never really knew what loving fully was. I learned to love out of responsibility or duty or because of tradition. Love was safe and comfortable.

But what if we could grow up learning what it means to love fully and then live the rest of our lives this way? Wouldn't that be even better than safe and comfortable? Is love really meant to be safe and comfortable all the time?

I believe not. I believe that love is meant to be 100 percent, not 50, 60, 70, 80, or even 90 percent. Loving 100 percent is not always comfortable. To love fully you have to risk sometimes.

Life is about loving fully, not holding back, but giving, believing, caring, showing, expressing, and being 100 percent love. That might sound romantic and idealistic, yet I believe that it is true. A friend recently was told that he was a hopeless romantic. He responded back that he was a hopeful romantic and he would rather love fully and risk than not love at all.

Life is about putting all of yourself into it. Life is about loving all the way, not part of the way because you are afraid of the other person's reaction, afraid of what someone might think, or afraid that they might not love you back as fully.

Don't hold back! Life is about loving fully and loving passionately! Life is about saying I love you fully rather than a quick "love you" at the end of a conversation. Loving fully means embracing your family and friends, cherishing and honoring your partner, and giving to your clients, your project, or your job.

Loving fully means doing things that make your heart pound, that make your stomach do back flips, that make your fingers and toes tingle. Loving fully means giving back to the world passionately all that you are so as to be a better you, live in a better world, and make a difference. Loving fully means taking risks, doing things you normally wouldn't do or things you've always wanted to do, and being 100 percent present and passionate.

Love fully and embrace love *now*! Don't hold back. You can never get—or give—too much love.

26. Take your time
and enjoy the ride.

*It is more important to know where you are going
than to get there quickly.*
~ Mabel Newcomber

"Take your time." Those words weren't even in my vocabulary up to a year ago. I wouldn't have known what they meant or how to go about even living that way. And even today I struggle with it, yet I am beginning to know better what they mean.

To me they mean stopping to take a breath, calling up a friend and finding out how they are doing, spending some time with myself, having fun once in a while, or not scheduling five things in one day for a change. I don't always do all those things, yet on this journey to live in the moment, I am finding that every day I learn a little bit more how to "enjoy the ride" with joy in my heart.

I am learning that taking my time sometimes results in a much better and more enjoyable outcome than rushing through and getting three, four, even ten things done. Sometimes it means doing one thing well and enjoying the ride, and other times it means doing a bunch of things to be able to experience getting done all the things on my list. Yet ultimately, it means not being in such a hurry all the darn time and just relaxing a bit and having more fun with life.

Is that really so hard? Either way, try it on for size and see how much better your moments are.

27. Surround yourself
with positive people.

Just as we can choose to eat well and exercise to keep our bodies healthy, we can choose to maintain positive energy by surrounding ourselves with positive people. People with negative energy can bring us down. People do not realize that they often hold others back or dim their inner light because of their own fears and insecurities. By holding those around them back, they may be lulled into a sense of complacency or comfort that they don't have it so bad. However, when friends and loved ones begin to thrive, it may often threaten their sense of complacency.

And those around us aren't the only thing holding us back. We're constantly bombarded with negative messages that we're not good enough or strong enough, that we're not partying enough or spending enough. We're just "not enough," according to all that blather and hype. To counteract the efforts by others to hold us back or dim our inner light, seek out people who will support you to be a better you, who challenge you to be more, do more, and make a difference. By surrounding yourself with this positive energy, you will find that you inspire yourself and others. Find new ways to appreciate, motivate, and support yourself and those around you so that we all can live more fully every moment.

28. FIGHT FOR A BETTER WORLD.

How wonderful it is that nobody need wait a single moment
before starting to improve the world.

~ ANNE FRANK

I love the message and the gift that Gandhi left the world.
Fighting does not always mean the brutal physical act of fighting.
It can also mean to strive to overcome adversity or to put forth
a determined effort to make something positive happen. People
fight for things and against things, but a personal fight is often the
struggle between not standing up and to fight or risking to make
the world a better place.

One of my goals "to fight for" is to touch one person, or one
being everyday so that their lives shine brighter than the day
before—to make a better world. With 365 days in the year, that
adds up to a much better world. In my world each day is a new
beginning and a new palette upon which to paint a legacy. That's
what I fight for.

What are the things that you are willing to fight for to make a
contribution, to make a better world? Now don't just think about
them. Today, take one action step toward making them happen!

29. Spend time with kids.

Kids are full of life, energy, vitality, and spontaneity. They see the world as one big *yes!* They want things *now*. They ask a million and one questions, especially *why?* They breathe fully; they live fully and from their heart. They have fun, they romp, they jump, they create, and they are curious. Kids remind us of all that is inside of us.

Over the years, the light that shines so bright from kids gets dimmed. We begin to put walls up, become afraid to do things—especially silly things—or take risks. Our fears become greater than our desires, and so we begin to get dull and accept what is comfortable rather than pursuing what our dreams promise.

Spending time with kids can revitalize this inner desire, passion, and penchant for dreaming. Being with kids forces us to be in our hearts rather than in our heads. It helps us to stay present to what is and what we want and entices us to go to that place of risking, being authentic, dreaming, and living fully.

The next time you feel stuck or even if you just want to remember what it was like to feel really alive, free, and excited about life—go hang out with some kids and really *be* with them.

30. SPEAK WITH SOMEONE
FROM ANOTHER COUNTRY.

Every time I go to another country or speak with someone from another country, it takes me outside of myself. The accent, the stories, the culture fill my mind.

In so many ways, I learn about new ways of thinking, being, and living. It makes me think about my life and the choices I am making. It gives me perspective on what else is happening in the world. It reminds me to stop and think about who I am and what I want in my life. It helps me to think and be in the now. I hear stories and I feel alive. I listen intently and am transported to other lives. Yet, at the same time I find that it also reminds me of my humanity—how connected I am to others and how connected we all are together. It helps me to remember to live fully now, to respect our differences and embrace our similarities.

If you get a chance, speak with someone from another country and see how it makes you feel.

31. ACCEPT A COMPLIMENT.

A compliment is something like
a kiss through a veil.
- VICTOR HUGO

We are often very willing, able, and capable of giving a compliment. Yet when we receive a compliment, we'll often shrug it off, or say "nah," or, "I know." Rarely do we gracefully accept the compliment with a simple "thank you" and own the truth of what the other person said. Why is this? Only you can know the answer.

Perhaps it is too hard for you to accept positive affirmations from others or believe what they said is really true. Whatever the case, make it a habit to accept compliments. Even make it a point to repeat it a few times to truly own and accept the truth of another person's words. Often times others see the qualities in us that we don't or can't even see in ourselves. Appreciate those, own those, and watch your perception of the universe expand.

32. ARRIVE EARLY.

How often do we rush around from here to there because we are late? Think about it! When I am late it leaves me no time to relax, take a breath and enjoy the moments in between. Nor does it allow me to take a minute when I arrive to settle in, prepare, or appreciate a connection or relationship.

Because I run around so frantically, I am habitually late or rushed, and because I rush, I create franticness. What kind of impact does this have on us? We live in a society and culture that is about getting things done, getting there fast, getting to the point and then moving on to the next thing.

I think what we are craving is to *be* instead of *doing* all the time. We are craving to *be* in relationships with other human beings, to *be* in the moment, to *be* connected, and to *be* at peace with ourselves and others. Instead, we get stuck "doing" all the time to the point that we are habitually late in all that we do. So perhaps the next time you have somewhere to get to, think about it as going somewhere to *be* and give yourself an extra few minutes to get there early and to just *be* for a few minutes before the doing gets started!

33. Take time for yourself.

*Learn to get in touch with the silence within yourself and know
that everything in this life has a purpose.*

~ Elisabeth Kubler-Ross

We live in a world that is "*woo* busy." There are cell phones,
e-mail, the Internet. There is fast food, packaged food, and take-
out. Every new invention is created to make everything more
convenient and faster to keep up with the pace of our lives. But
what happens is instead of everything getting more convenient,
the pace just keeps speeding up like an avalanche picking up speed
as it tumbles downhill.

An avalanche starts off with a little piece of snow breaking off
a mountainside, but it quickly turns into a massive wave of snow
plunging downward, destroying anything and everything in the
way. This is how our lives and world are becoming. The technology,
the gadgets, the resources started out being useful, everyday tools
to help us become more efficient and effective in our lives. Yet
now they have completely turned the pace of our lives to full tilt.
People have access to us at any and all times and in every part of
the world. No time is sacred.

There is no such thing as "alone" time anymore. Someone can always track us down—that is if we let them. If we don't specifically take time for ourselves, we may be run into the ground with "busy-ness." Yet if we find the time to spend alone to recharge, we are better able to regenerate. Then we can use all those tools and resources toward a positive end.

Taking time out for ourselves allows us to heal, to breathe, and to be. Even if it is just for a few minutes every day, an hour once a week, or an evening once a month, take some time out for yourself to recharge and see how much more fun and effective you will be when you go back to the fast pace of life!

34. PUT YOUR STAKE IN THE GROUND.

When you put your stake in the ground, you are saying to the world: this is what I believe. It is taking a stand on something regardless of what people say. It is personal integrity. I have been so blessed in my life to have silent teachers who always put their stake in the ground without expectation of recognition for their contribution. In history there are many leaders who have put their stake in the ground, and in our own time, there are many leaders that have taken a stand and made a difference for humanity.

No matter what my father did or did not do, he had one consistent trait. He kept his own counsel. He didn't deviate from what he believed, and he made sure that I understood this about him.

When I was a teenager living in Louisiana, my father was involved with research at the leprosy hospital in Carville. On weekends, my father would bring home one of the residents from the facility. I looked forward to these weekend visits from strangers to our home. They were amazing people with great stories that filled our home all weekend. They were just like us except that society determined they should be locked away. He wanted me to experience these "outcasts," to find out that they were people too, and it didn't matter what anyone did or said about it. So, in keeping with this tradition, I urge you to open your heart and take a stand. Put your stake the ground with love and passion for what you believe in and stand for.

35. WRITE IN A JOURNAL.

I have been writing in a journal for a long time. I recently moved, and as I was packing up my books, I realized I had a stack of about fifteen journals. Wow! I never realized how much I wrote in a journal. Now, don't get me wrong, not all of those journals are completely filled up. Leave it to an Aquarius to start many journals and get about half-way to three- quarters through and want to start a new one!

However, it was pretty amazing to see all those journals and know that I wrote them. As I looked through them, they demonstrated the ebbs and flows of my life. There are a lot of ups and downs, and often times I found that I wrote in journals more when I was down than when I was up—pretty interesting. That is, until recently. Lately, I learned the art of writing every day for at least five minutes a day, no matter what, the good, the bad, and the ugly. What I also committed to is writing more about the positive, about what is going well in my life, about the good things I've accomplished, about the things that I am grateful and happy for. It makes a *big* difference.

For many people, writing in a journal may seem tedious or boring. Yet, what I would recommend to you is give it at least thirty days of writing in your journal at some point during the day every day, but shoot for 101 days! It is like exercise. While we have the best intention of exercising every day, getting started is always the hardest part. However, once you create a routine it gets easier.

Why is it that we are willing to exercise our body, yet we aren't willing to do the same to nurture our mind and creativity? Think of journaling like exercising. The beginning is the hardest part. Yet once we get started, it is amazing what begins to come and be created in our lives. Writing in a journal can serve to clear your mind and set yourself up for a great day. It can serve to wash away a busy and hectic day and help you go to bed grateful and calm. Or it can be a good break in the middle of the day from the hubbub of life. Whatever the case may be, give it a try. Write in a journal every day for 101 days and see how much better you feel!

36. Don't worry.

Worry is interest paid on trouble before it falls due.
~ Dean William R. Inge

Why do we worry so much? We are a society that worries about everything. I see people worry about their health, their work, their kids, their family, their happiness, their life, their friends, the weather, the world...you get they picture. They worry about everything.

I come from a long line of worriers. It seems as though not a minute ever goes by in which they aren't worrying about something. My family is not alone in this. I see this happening in the world all around me. Sometimes I even find myself worrying about this, that, and the other thing. In the meantime, I am missing out on what is right now because I'm so worried about what will be. When I do this, I have to stop and remind myself to live for the now and appreciate the moments I have today.

Next time you find yourself worrying, find something in the present to focus on and appreciate, and just let go of the worry.

37. Be happy.

There is no duty we so much underrated
as the duty of being happy. By being happy
we sow anonymous benefits upon the world.
~ Robert Louis Stevenson

"Don't Worry….Be Happy," by Bobby McFerrin and "Every Little Thing Gonna be Alright" by Bob Marley played over and over on my son's iPod as I sat holding him while he was having a biopsy on his hand. We even sang along with gusto as we waited for the pathology evaluation.

This was a scary time, but as I listened to happy music, it put me into a happy state. I focused on the beauty of my son and all the happiness I share with him. My eyes welled with emotional tears of joy as I allowed happiness to fill my heart. I felt light, and so did he.

It is our choice, in every day and in every moment, to be happy. When we choose to be happy, we elevate our energetic vibrations so we do not constantly fear the moment. We're living in it so it just "is." Choose to be happy. Share happiness with everyone you meet today and you might find that there really was something to Bobby McFerrin's song!

38. Do not take life too seriously.

Do not take life too seriously.
You will never get out of it alive.
~ Elbert Hubbard

It is scary when we make something so big and powerful that we are paralyzed by the thought of moving away from the event or the experience. While it is always good to hold a vision of what we want, if we become too serious about it, we can get stuck. If we get serious when we think something should look a certain way or a person should act a certain way, then we're not able to be creative, to be open to the possibilities of other outcomes.

When I get too serious about something, my body stops feeling good. My stomach starts churning into knots, my chest tightens, my breathing becomes shallow, and my thoughts get cloudy. When I'm in the midst of an event or experience, and I allow it to become so serious that it controls me, I'm the one that loses. Once the event has passed, I realize it wasn't so important.

This can happen every day. Life, Karma, The Law, call it what you will, has a way of healing us—in spite of our control. Yesterday, as I watched outside my window, a beautiful bird landed upon a new plant my husband had placed in the front yard. As I commented on the beauty of this new bird, my husband frantically ran outside toward the plant. I didn't know why he did it until later. The bird had taken the monarch butterfly cocoon that was growing on the new plant and the cocoon killed the bird. (Monarch butterfly cocoons are poisonous.) My husband tried to control that outcome, but he couldn't, and we both had to not get too serious about what just happened.

There is a delicate balance in life. Enjoy the beauty that is your life and your experience. Be open to accepting what happens and never get too serious about any of it!

39. Ski, ride, bike, or climb.

Any extreme outdoor activity demands focus and discipline and requires being 100 percent in the moment. If you don't stay present then you can slip and fall, crash into a tree, or otherwise hurt or dismember yourself. These activities remind and teach you to truly live in the present. The intense focus helps to keep you in the present, rather than thinking about the past or future.

If you find yourself stuck in the past or thinking about the future and unable to be present, get outdoors and do an activity that keeps you focused on the present. If nothing else it is a gift you can give yourself today to give your mind time to catch up.

40. Take the time for a pause.

The notes I handle no better than many pianists. But the pause
between the notes—ah, that is where the art resides.

~ Artur Schnabel

Rarely do we have a few minutes, let alone a few hours, to really take the time to pause and look inward—to get to know ourselves, get in touch with who we are and what we really want out of life. At least once in your life, and preferably once a year, go out and spend twenty-four hours somewhere in a favorite place (camping, by a fire, or otherwise) without television, radio, computers, iPods, cell phones, books, or other distractions and get in touch with yourself. Bring a journal and pen. Take lots of walks, and just take the time to take a break and get in touch with yourself, your life, and what you want. Spend some time contemplating how you can better appreciate the journey.

Use this as a starting point to discover where you want to go and to identify opportunities for living fully. In subsequent sessions, use the time as a check-in point to measure where you are in relation to your dreams, where your life and goals may have shifted, and if and how you have been enjoying the journey. Then re-chart your course to stay on track with your inner voice and get busy living. You will find when you take these pauses that you are invigorated, recharged, and able to take on the world.

41. Progress not perfection.

Perfection consists not in doing extraordinary things,
but in doing ordinary things extraordinarily well.

~ Angelique Arnauld

I could write books about this expression and quote. Perfection is what I used to strive for every day. How tiring and exhausting that life was for me. Recently, I was given the label of being a "Patty Perfect." How appropriate, how fitting! It truly was eye opening for me to see that others saw me as a perfectionist too.

Why did I have such a need to be perfect, to get it right, to do it perfectly all the time? I was always setting myself up for failure because perfection doesn't exist. Because I wanted "perfect," I would always strive to do better or more, but being labeled a "Patty Perfect," the question became "then what?" I could always find ways to criticize myself for not getting it right or focus on what I still had to do or what I could do better.

Is this any way to live? I think not, yet, it is the way I have chosen to live so much of my life. I know that I have always tried to measure up to some standard but never quite seemed to make it. Yet I kept on trying—striving for the unattainable and being pretty miserable in the process. So when I first heard this saying, "progress not perfection," it was such a relief to me. You mean, I could do things a little bit at a time, at my own pace, not necessarily to perfection, and I would be okay? Heck yeah! I wouldn't just be okay; I'd be a lot happier better than if I continually tried to be perfect!

Don't get me wrong, I still strive for excellence, but when I get too caught up in being perfect, I miss all the moments, the opportunities, and life's little gifts. As I learn to move along, live life honestly, and march to my own beat, life is a lot more fun, a lot more real, and a lot happier! Next time you find yourself caught up in getting it perfect, let go, have fun with whatever you're doing, and enjoy the moment.

42. Prepare a gourmet meal.

A great meal is like a fireworks display,
nothing remains.

~ Paul Bocuse

It starts with the crackle of garlic hitting the olive oil in the pan and then its distinctive smell wafting through the air. This is the beginning of almost any meal in Italy, a country where home, family, and community are centerpiece of the culture. The time and energy that goes into preparing the meal is a labor—and gift—of love. It often begins at the market with a quest for the freshest ingredients. Then comes the washing, cutting, rolling, soaking, pounding, dousing, mixing, combining, separating, frying, sautéing, simmering, boiling, baking, grilling, and sprinkling of carefully selected ingredients. Every step of this process takes care, attention, and passion.

I have visions of my *Nonna* (grandmother, in Italian) spending hours in the kitchen preparing our meals with love, adoration, and affection. It was an all-day affair that often involved a lot of busy time chopping or mixing. Yet it also involved a lot of downtime while waiting for the ingredients to simmer together to fuse the flavors in a magical way. These breaks were her opportunity to go into the other room and spend time reading, learning a language, or sharing her stories of wisdom and love with us kids.

Meals are the centerpiece of many cultures. However in today's fast-paced American society, it has become harder and harder to invest the same energy, time, and love into a meal. When we do prepare a gourmet meal with painstaking care and attention, it can truly bring us back into the moment of *now*.

I find that when I prepare a gourmet meal, I get into each moment. I lose track of other things and become truly present and focused. For me, preparing a gourmet meal isn't just about eating, which I admit I like very much. It's about sharing the experience with others—the food's flavors, textures, aromas, as well as the conversation and relationships between friends. It reminds me to be present and enjoy the little things, and it completely takes my mind off of anything outside that moment.

Try taking some time to prepare a gourmet meal from start to finish and share it with the people you love. It might actually bring you back to appreciating the little things.

43. VISIT FRIENDS OR FAMILY.

A friend is someone who sees through you
and still enjoys the view.

~ WILMA ASKINAS

Visiting, whether friends or family, is near and dear to my being alive and living fully. From my visits, I feel such love and laughter. I have a friend whom I adore and have known for over twenty years. We see one another less often than we would like. However, the moment we connect, it's as if no time has passed. We still have a great time, just like when we were twenty-something with little responsibility. We stay up all night, talking and dreaming, listening and crying.

There is a beauty in connecting with a friend or family member that transcends words: a place where the heart becomes light and understands all. It is this place that gives our lives the sweet fragrance of memory that connects us to each other.

44. Chocolate works
for just about anything.

Hot chocolate, milk chocolate, dark chocolate, hazelnut chocolate, white chocolate, ginger chocolate, chocolate truffles, chocolate cake, chocolate bars, chocolate ice cream, chocolate kisses, chocolate fudge, chocolate chips, chocolate cookies, chocolate brownies, smores–n–chocolate, chocolate liquor, nutella, chocolate sauce, chocolate cream pie, chocolate-dipped ice cream, Mexican chocolate, Swiss chocolate, Italian chocolate, Belgian chocolate, chocolate mint, chocolate chunks, chocolate bon bons, chocolate fondu, chocolate bundt cake, chocolate bark, chocolate with almonds…

Chocolate, chocolate, chocolate…have I got your attention? I thought so! How wonderful is chocolate? Chocolate is great for any occasion and all occasions! How much fun is chocolate? Chocolate is one of my favorite things. Now I don't recommend going overboard (unless of course this is what your intuition is telling you!); however, chocolate has a way of adding a little something special to life. If you ever need a pick-me-up or something to shift your mood, pop a chocolate truffle in your mouth and enjoy the moment.

Great chocolate is an orgasmic experience. It is creamy and infuses my mouth with sensations, textures, and pleasure. I always buy the best chocolate money can buy, and I've searched the world for the best. I like to take a bite, close my eyes, and become one with an experience that totally takes me out of my physical self into a world of possibilities. Knowing I can have this experience with chocolate inspires me to have this experience everywhere in my life. It is food and nourishment from the divine.

45. Believe in yourself.

This is the most amazing gift I have ever given myself, my family, and the world. It sounds a bit hokey, yet how often do we go through life not believing in ourselves? Think about the last time you really believed you were worthy or beautiful, talented or wise.

Deep inside each of us is a feeling place. Sometimes we call it a hunch. Some people call it a gut feeling or intuition. I think of it as my connection to the divine—the source that is always there for me, always supporting and loving me. The goal is to first love yourself and believe you are "enough" for all the good and beautiful things in your life. Be willing to let go of the things that no longer serve you. Trust that you know the answers. You do, because your answers are contained within you. Take the time to believe in yourself and your life will bloom with pure abundance.

46. Go with the flow.

Let things flow naturally forward
in whatever way they like.

~ Lao Tsu

Just recently I had the perfect day to practice being in the moment. I arrived late to my client's office and when I dropped off my car, there were no parking spots. Thankfully the parking attendant said he could double-park me. He then took my keys and reminded me to come back by 2:00 p.m. before he left for the day. At 1:00 p.m. I reminded myself to go move my car before 2:00 p.m. At 3:30 p.m. I realized I had forgotten to get my keys as I was packing up to go to another meeting.

Now normally I would have really been stressed out, but this time I decided that everything was going to work out and I would just go with the flow—what else could I do? So I decided to take the shuttle to my 4:00 p.m. meeting and at that meeting I would find someone to drive me to my 5:30 p.m. meeting. That's exactly what happened. Then when I got to that meeting, I found someone who was willing to drive me home to pick up my spare keys and then back to my car! I couldn't believe how beautifully everything worked out. It was my intention that it would work, and that is how it went!

What a *big* realization it was for me to just let go and accept what was. Once I decided it would be okay, I just literally let the rest of the day work itself out. It was that easy—plain and simple. I really understood how we tend to make things so much more difficult than they have to be! So the next time you get into a difficult spot, look for the solutions and options, but don't get upset. Decide it will work out and then have a good attitude, go with the flow, and see where it takes you!

47. PLAY HOOKY...

...if for no other reason than to spend the day with yourself. Remember how much fun it was to play hooky in school? It still is really fun! I remember one fall day last year; I had been having a really rough couple of weeks, and I had committed to go to a conference on a Friday afternoon. It was a crystal clear Colorado day, and I had just had it. So I decided to play hooky. Rather than putting on my suit and heading to the conference, I decided to put on my cycling gear, jump on my bike, and go for a ride! How refreshing!

I felt like a kid again. Instead of being indoors on this beautiful day, I was spinning around the park, taking in the fresh air and watching all the other people who were also probably playing hooky. I felt so alive, revived, and rejuvenated. In playing hooky, I realized I needed to free up a bit more time to just let go of some of my responsibilities and have some fun. It's freeing to say, "What the heck," every once in a while. When was the last time you played hooky?

48. Sometimes put down
the list.

*We must be willing to let go of the life we have planned
so as to have the life that is waiting for us.*
~ Joseph Campbell

I'm sure you've figured out by now that up until just recently, I have always planned my life. Literally, I create "to-do" lists for everything because I forget things, and I feel like lists are the only way that I can keep myself on track. So I make lists. I plan every minute of the day, every hour of the week, and every day of the year. It is a rare occasion that I do not plan out everything I am going to say or do. And while planning may often be a good thing as it helps me get things done, it also can be quite limiting.

Planning often prevents me from being in the moment because I am *beholden to the list*—and that's the problem. The list keeps me from being spontaneous because I always have something to do. It also keeps me from really living and experiencing the moments that make life so special.

This is part of why I decided to write this book—to take a look at the things that I am doing well and to correct or change direction when I am off course. Now don't get me wrong, I will still make lists and plan. However, what I am learning by writing this book is that I don't have to plan so much. Sometimes I can just let go and let things come to me. When I find the balance between planning and letting go, life gets a whole lot easier and more fun.

The next time you have the choice between doing something you have on your "to-do" list and just doing something unplanned, put down the list and take a break. You don't have to put the list down every time, yet you might find that by putting it down some of the time, it allows you to appreciate more fully life's special moments and helps you to be even more productive the rest of the time.

49. DISCONNECT FROM

TECHNOLOGY.

Technology...the knack of so arranging the world
that we don't have to experience it.

~ MAX FRISCH

Technology is an amazing gift. It connects us to anything, anytime, and anywhere. But it also has a downside. If you stay constantly connected, you stay frantic. It seems that unless we're forced to disconnect from the rat-race, we never have moments of downtime.

About a year ago we had an earthquake in Hawaii, and for more than a day we were cut off from technology of every kind. After the earth shook audibly for over a minute, everything associated with technology was silenced and something marvelous happened. We talked to neighbors we had not spoken with for some time. We shared laughter and *ohana,* or community, in Hawaii. The best part was when darkness set in. The stars were brighter than usual because there was total darkness, total silence. This involuntary disconnect was an amazing gift, and it taught me that I periodically need to make a conscious decision to disconnect from technology.

It is so easy to get caught up in the world and all the "stuff" we need to do. When I disconnect consciously, it allows me to refuel. Schedule a day regularly to disconnect from technology, reconnect with yourself, and feel the gratitude for life.

50. GO FOR A WALK.

It is good to collect things, but it is better to go on walks.

~ ANATOLE FRANCE

This is my gift. Walking is pure connection with the divine. I am both blessed and grateful to live near the ocean. The sound of the waves is an invitation, a reminder for me to take time in the present moment and experience all that the ocean can give. A walk on the beach for me is magical. As my feet leave the comfort of my slippers and touch the cool tiny pebbles of sand, my presence begins to shift. It is as if I've been transported into presence. I become the sand. With eyes closed and the trade winds moving my body, I become aware of my impermanence. I become the wind, strong and constantly changing. I become the ocean. I am present.

Walking involves an awareness of our senses and grounds us to the earth. It is one of our most basic and inherent experiences. Walking in awareness, no matter where it is, creates a sense of presence, of being present.

I know people who are not physically able to walk; however, in their mind's eye, they imagine walking and experience the same connection with the the earth. Go for a walk; connect to your presence. For in connecting to presence, we find the divine. In finding our connection with the divine, we find our true essence. We find ourselves.

51. Choose love over fear.

So much of my life I have found myself living in and paralyzed by fear. We are a society living in fear. The media, the politicians, and just about every societal message around us tends to perpetuate a victim or fear-based consciousness. Why is this so? What can we do to overcome this?

For me the answer has been to let go of the fear and being afraid. I have begun to choose love over a life of living in fear. That may seem Pollyanna-ish or simplistic, yet it really is that simple. It is a choice. We can choose to live in fear, to be afraid of every choice, to be worried about what others are going to do. If we take that route, we're making it likely that what we fear will actually come to be. Or we can choose to focus on being loving, caring, and giving human beings.

As I begin to love more and see the love in others, I find that is what comes back to me. It is that whole law-of-attraction thing— the more we choose love over fear, the more love comes back to us. The next time you find yourself afraid or paralyzed by fear, let it go, switch, and just come from a space of love. Choose to love, to be loving, and you will be loved back.

52. ASK AND YOU SHALL RECEIVE.

How often do we really ask for what we want? As a child I asked for everything—don't we all? But none of us got everything we wanted. In fact, because we got told no too much, we often stopped asking. I think somewhere in my adolescence, I came to some conclusion that if I really wanted something it would just come to me. If it didn't, I just thought that it wasn't meant to be. Little did I know that if I didn't ask for something, it wouldn't just appear.

The result for me was that at some point in my life, I became very unclear about what I even wanted anymore. I also became afraid of asking because I was afraid of getting the answer no.

Recently I have started to ask again for the things I want. Sometimes it's with big things, and other times it's with little things. I recently got a divorce and turned to friends. I just asked if they would be there for me when I needed to cry or needed a hug. I asked if they would help me move. I asked if they would support me. Because I found that people were willing to say yes instead of no, I got some courage. I then asked for an interview with a famous person for an idea I am working on. I realized that if I didn't ask, I almost certainly would not receive.

I am finally seeing that when I do ask, I often get what I want. When I don't get it, I don't take it personally. Instead, I learn from it and think about how I could ask or do something a little differently next time.

When you get a chance to ask for something, ask. Don't take the opportunity away from someone else to give you what you ask for. Don't ever make the assumption that someone won't want to help you or do what you ask. It's their choice, not yours, to say *no*. Besides, what have you got to lose? "You never know until you ask," is an old saying, and it's true. If you ask and you don't get, isn't that better than not asking at all? If you never ask, then you never know what you might have gotten, and you might steal the opportunity for someone else to give to you.

53. TURN OFF THE TELEVISION.

Television is democracy at it's ugliest.

~ PADDY CHAYEFSKY

Living in prime time—much of our society here in the West relaxes in front of the TV. We sit; our bodily functions to slow, and we slowly become unconscious. In front of the TV, our dreams and imagination cease. We easily slip into someone else's dreams and imagination, but this transportation of our being can stifle our potential and shield us from our purpose.

Turn your TV off for just one week. Experience yourself, and hear sounds you might not otherwise hear when the TV is occupying your sound space. See beauty that may have escaped your sight. Really taste the food you offer your body. Smell the aroma of your surroundings. Feel the energy of your material surroundings, and sense the spiritual force that is you. Rediscover your own creativity and imagination—and maybe you'll just decide to leave that darn thing off.

54. Pick a flower.

The late blooming flowers are the prettiest
and the longest lasting.
~ John Scholfield

Pick a flower on earth and you move the farthest star.
~ Paul Dirac

I remember one time I had taken a walk and saw a patch of flowers that were totally unique. I went home that night and felt the flowers calling to me. So I went back that night and picked one to remind me of the beauty and the uniqueness of that day.

There is nothing like the feeling of seeing a beautiful flower, picking it, and taking it home to enjoy for yourself. Even better is if you are randomly coming home one night and decide to stop and pick a flower for your friend, partner, or loved ones. You don't have to wait to do it for a special occasion either. I think it's better to just give someone a flower spontaneously on some random day of the week.

Surprise your loved one or treat yourself to the gift of a freshly-picked flower. It can serve as a reminder of how unique, perfectly created, and special we all are! When you are driving home some night or taking a walk, stop by the side of the road and pick a wild flower that you like!

55. Focus on the solution, not the problem.

How often do we focus on problems instead of solutions? It is relatively amusing for me to think about how often I do this. It really isn't rocket science. When we hit a fork in the road or an obstacle along the way, rather than focusing on the obstacle, how easy would it be to just look for solutions or other options that are available?

The solutions in life are limitless if we are open to them and actively look for them. I have found that I often focused on the problem because I really wasn't open to or didn't want the solution. Now I am beginning to understand that if I really want something, I have to have 100 percent clear intention to find a solution. I have found that when I think this way, no matter what obstacles get in my way, I will find a way to solve my problem because I will be open to the solutions and what is possible rather than what is impossible.

If you get stuck, let go of the problems and obstacles; look for new options and solutions, and see how easy life can be.

56. Smile.

You've got a lot of choices. If getting out of bed
in the morning is a chore and you're not smiling
on a regular basis, try another choice.
~ Steven D. Woodhull

Smile, even hint a smile, and your energy changes. If you're down, it's okay to fake it at first. Even if it feels strange or awkward, smile because something magical happens when you do. Your body starts to respond with joy and peace. Try it now. Close your eyes and frown. What do you feel? Now smile, just a little at first, and feel the shift of energy in your body. Now give a *big* smile, so big you think it might hurt. It doesn't, does it? It feels *good!* Do it more and more, especially when you catch yourself falling into a frown. When in doubt, just smile! ☺

I remember as a child I had a poster that said, "Smile, it gives your face something to do." I had it hanging prominently in my room where I could look at it every day. It worked; it triggered me to smile. Amazing how something that simple could make a smile happen.

Think about how you feel when you smile. Think about the moments when you are feeling down, but give even the littlest bit of a smile and *bam!*—your mood shifts. I have heard it said that it takes fewer muscles to smile than it does to frown. So we must be real gluttons for punishment if we are frowning more than we are smiling. The next time you find yourself frowning, stop for a moment and think of something that will make you smile and watch how the rest of you lights up as your face does.

57. Be uncomfortable.

Be willing to be uncomfortable.
Be comfortable being uncomfortable. It may get tough,
but it's a small price to pay for living a dream.
~ Peter McWilliams

Being uncomfortable is about change. Being uncomfortable is also about achieving your dreams. You have to be willing to be uncomfortable if you want to live your dreams.

I am realizing more and more every day that as I dare to dream more and more in my life, I have more uncomfortable moments. Now I can let this discomfort lull me into complacency and prevent me from taking the necessary steps toward my dreams, or I can choose to be okay with feeling uncomfortable. I can get comfortable feeling uncomfortable. I can allow myself to feel uncomfortable and not beat myself up about it. The more often I do this and ride the wave of discomfort, the more quickly it passes.

What are the dreams you are striving for? Are they worth being uncomfortable for? As you reach for your dreams, be okay with being uncomfortable, and always remember to keep taking the next step!

58. Take the T.

In tennis there is an expression of "taking the T." If you look at a tennis court from a bird's-eye view, you'll see a prominent upside down "T." When you take tennis lessons, you learn that you start the game in the center, right in the crook of the "T," because it is the most strategic place on the court to be able to handle anything that comes your way.

The translation for life is starting your day by setting the day right. I used to wake up and run out the door to go swim or exercise. I always checked my e-mail first thing. Starting my day this way was merely a reaction or a response to others, so I was never guiding my own life and dictating how I wanted my day to go. I was responding to others and starting from where they took me, not where I led myself. This kept me off track and following another's path.

Today when I wake up, I meditate, visualize, or begin writing to start my day. This way I am mentally and emotionally setting up my day according to my values, not those of others. It makes all the difference in the world in allowing me to respond to the world rather than reacting and letting others pull me off track. Whether it is writing, meditating, or some other proactive action every morning, start your day by "taking the T" and see how every day becomes your day instead of a day driven by others.

59. Pamper yourself and enjoy it.

*Any little bit of experimenting in self-nurturance
is very frightening for most of us.*

~ Julia Cameron

I love to pamper myself. I do it very well. I once had a boyfriend who said something I shall never forget: "You buy yourself nice things, don't you?" I was so caught off guard by the question that it has remained with me.

You see, I was raised by two beautiful women. "Mammy" was soft, large, loving, and always cooking, cleaning, or working in the farm. She never, in my memory, did anything for herself. Mammy did for everyone else. My "Auntie" was totally opposite. She was clean and always well groomed from the moment she got out of bed in the morning until we all retired for the evening. Every Saturday she went to the beauty shop and had her hair done. She painted her nails, took a bath every day, and taught me to do the same. After my bath, I got to use her nice-smelling powder all over my body, and I sparkled like a princess. Not only did I feel special, I really liked myself and I felt *good!*

I pamper myself everyday because I want to feel good but also so that I can share my goodness with everyone I meet.

A few years ago, I spent some time in France. The experience only reinforced the positive memories I developed as a child about being and pampering myself. Always pamper yourself and enjoy being you!

I remember the first time I pampered myself and actually enjoyed it. I was in my mid-twenties, and I had never treated myself to anything that would be considered pampering. I didn't even know what that word meant. I had been so trained to make everything in life functional that pampering myself hadn't even crossed my mind. Even when I first started to learn that I could pamper myself and I was taught how to do it, I never really enjoyed it. Yeah, I did it—meaning I went through the motions, but I wasn't really getting pampered.

It wasn't until recently that I actually just went with it and enjoyed the moment of being pampered. That is, I stayed present in the pampering and stopped thinking about everything but the pampering. I stopped worrying about all the things I still had to get done or what I didn't do well enough the day before. I stopped pondering what I should do or be when I grew up. And I finally just stopped and enjoyed being pampered. What a concept!

Next time you get a chance to go do something to pamper yourself, go for it. And this isn't just for women. Men, too, get out there and do something to pamper yourself, and make sure you don't just go through the motions. Relax and enjoy the ride!

60. Take photographs.

Photographs actually stop time and preserve memories. The speed of light is 186,000 miles per second, and the shutter speed on a camera is one hundredth of a second. Life happens moment by moment. By taking photographs, moments are captured, frozen, so that they can be examined, shared, preserved, and above all remembered.

I have a friend who is photographer, and when I asked him about taking photos, this is what he wrote:

> *When I am shooting a wedding, and the minister pronounces, "I now pronounce you man and wife. You may now kiss the bride," that moment takes a fraction of a second. Yet, when I am there and I take a photo, then that fraction of a second is preserved for the man and woman, for their living family, for their unborn children and grandchildren and so on and so forth into perpetuity.*

Taking photographs acknowledges that *right now* time is being stopped and a special moment is being preserved. Through a photograph, it is possible to control light and capture whatever the mind sees so that the moment is preserved to share with everyone. What a better way to live in the moment than by taking a photograph, being truly in the moment, and then preserving that moment?

61. Take your watch off.

Have you ever taken your watch off for a few hours or even for a whole day, but you check the spot on your arm where you watch is about every ten minutes? There is some statistic about how often we check our watches every day, and it is something like 1,000 times. I know it sounds crazy, yet it is probably true!

As Americans, we are so tied to what time it is. I do it all the time. I get fixated on what I have to do, when I have to do it, and where I have to be at what time. I am a slave to my watch, and this is probably true for many other people too.

So what can we do about it? I'm not sure if there is any silver bullet. However, I have found that when I don't wear my watch at least once a month, it frees me from the requirements and expectations that automatically come with wearing a watch. That doesn't mean I don't still do things and go places. It just means I become a little more relaxed and less uptight about how much I have to get done and when and where I have to be. It also frees me to be a bit more in the moment. It allows me to be a bit less worried about what is coming next and to appreciate what is going on right now.

Go ahead; take your watch off and see how it frees you.

62. Empathize.

The great gift of human beings is that
we have the power of empathy.

~ Meryl Streep

Empathy is the ability to identify with and understand another's situation, feelings, and motives. Empathy is the cornerstone of humanity. If we are able to empathize with others, we may begin to feel our connectedness to humanity, our oneness. When we empathize we begin to not feel so alone. Often times when I am in a bad mood or a funky space, all I have to do to snap back into the moment and into a better frame of mind is to put myself in another person's shoes.

Taking myself outside of myself into the world, thoughts, feelings, or lives of others enables me to see the bigger picture. It reminds me that I am part of a bigger universe. It allows me to relax for a moment and just be present where I am at now—not judging others, nor criticizing myself, but recognizing my humility and my humanity. It can give me a lot of perspective and understanding.

Empathize with others and watch a whole new world open up to you.

63. JUST BE.

"Just do it" was a famous marketing motto in the 1990s—an expression that epitomizes the twentieth century. We have now entered the twenty-first century, and it is time to stop doing so much and actually start being once in a while. How much more amazing would our lives and our planet be if we could stop doing all the time and just be?

I have worked in public policy for over ten years and I see a flurry of doing every day. I have studied, researched, and spent time in communities working on social change and action. One thing continues to stick out. As a society we are all so focused on *doing*, we have forgotten how to *be*.

In education, I see the commoditization of our children: give them more tests to be more accountable so they can be a more productive workforce. In health, I see a flurry of diseases, mental health problems, and substance-abuse issues plaguing people as they scurry to do more, have more, or achieve more, but they have forgotten how to just be, to take care of themselves first. Socially, I have watched as our society chooses to spend more on jails and locking people away rather than on ensuring our children have good educations or access to early, preventive health care.

When are we going to recognize that as things have gotten busier and as we strive to do more that we are becoming less happy and healthy? When are we going to see that our productivity, our health, and our wellness as individuals, as a society, and ultimately as humanity, depends on us slowing down a little bit, rejuvenating, taking care of ourselves, and just *being* once in a while?

Over the past six months I have witnessed a number of friends battle cancer, heart disease, and other life-threatening illnesses. I can't help but believe it is because we are increasingly becoming an out-of-alignment society. We are caught up in the doing and have forgotten how to be.

I, myself, have been guilty of this throughout much of my life. I believe it is one of the main reasons that I have suffered from many illnesses. Yet as I have embarked on a journey of living more fully in the moment, I find I am healthier and happier every day.

When was the last time you took time for yourself to just be? It may just be what you need to heal, to be happy, and to live fully.

64. ACKNOWLEDGE OTHERS.

When you acknowledge others, you're telling them that who they are or what they've done is okay. But as I've worked to acknowledge others, I have discovered something intriguing. For a long time, I was not able to acknowledge others because somehow I didn't think I was worthy enough or good enough to acknowledge myself. I realize now that it was never about others. It was about my own inner struggle to acknowledge myself. If I didn't feel I deserved it, I would have a hard time allowing others to deserve it as well.

I am now learning that no matter what space I am in, whether I am on top of the world feeling confident, comfortable, or secure in myself, or if I am feeling insecure and undeserving, I still acknowledge others on a regular basis. I find that it helps me to be present and appreciate who they are and often times serves as a reminder to myself of all that I am as well.

The next time you are feeling as though you don't want to acknowledge someone for something they have accomplished, that is all the more reason to go ahead and do so. By acknowledging them, you are not only telling them that they're okay, you're sending a message deep down to yourself that you're okay as well. It is a gift to both you and them. And I think that sometimes, the gift you give yourself by acknowledging another is greater than the one you're giving them.

135

65. Feel.

Never apologize for showing feeling.
When you do so, you apologize for the truth.
~ Benjamin Disraeli

The visceral thing is called emotion...and well, if we didn't have
it, none of all this really would be worthwhile.
~ Michael Tucker

I have finally opened up to feeling. It only took me thirty-something years. I remember when I graduated from college, I moved to Atlanta. At one point, my father came to take care of me because I had surgery. It felt really good. He cared for me, cooked for me, and made sure that I was healing. I distinctly remember when I was driving him to the airport on his last day, he turned to me in the car and told me that *Nonno* (my Italian grandfather) had died. I became very emotional, but he turned and said, "No, don't worry; there is no need to cry." I was sad. Why wasn't it okay for me to feel my emotions, to let them out and grieve the loss of my grandfather?

In society today, this is how so many of us are raised. At some point, holding our emotions in begins to kill us. I know for me, in my early twenties I finally had an emotional breakdown and cried off and on for nearly six months. Every opportunity I got, I cried. Within the next few years, I had several serious health conditions emerge even though I was very young. To this day, I am convinced it is because I finally allowed myself to feel and release all of the emotions I had been holding in. As I allowed my emotions to come out, I released all the toxins and disease within me that had developed from holding it all inside.

It wasn't until recently that I truly began to feel. I realized that I had stuffed away so many of my feelings for so long. What a relief to feel and allow myself to feel! Every day now I am more and more grateful for all the emotions I have. I no longer suppress them and hold them back. I let them come as they are—good or bad. With hurt, sadness, anger and frustration, I am finding that the sooner I feel these emotions and allow myself to feel, the quicker they blow through me. If I hold them in, the more resentful I grow! On the other end of the spectrum is joy, happiness, love, and fun. This is what life is all about—feeling!

Recently my friend, Michael, shared with me his quote on emotions that I cited above. How true it is! Life is about feeling, breathing, jumping in, and living! Without the ups and downs and all-arounds, life would be pretty boring and wouldn't really be worthwhile! So make sure to really and truly allow yourself to feel!

66. THINK POSITIVE THOUGHTS.

You can't expect to prevent negative feelings altogether. And you can't expect to experience positive feelings all the time. The Law of Emotional Choice directs us to acknowledge our feelings but also to refuse to get stuck in the negative ones.

~ GREG ANDERSON

That quote really says it all. We all have negative thoughts, but do we ever realize how much negativity we create from our thinking? I never fully realized how many negative thoughts I had until I started paying more careful attention to what I was thinking throughout the day. It amazed me.

Now the quote does not say not to have negative thoughts or, if you do, to suppress those thoughts. That would not be healthy. What it is saying is that we have a choice when we do have negative thoughts. We can acknowledge the negative thought, let the thought pass through us so we're not stuck in it, and then think of a positive thought with which to replace the negative one.

It really is that simple: when you have a negative thought, immediately think of something positive to replace the negative one. We are our thoughts, and our thoughts create our realities. So if we are thinking negatively, then we will remain in a negative space until something shifts. We can let time shift us naturally, but sometimes that takes a really long time. Or we can shift ourselves by immediately thinking of something positive. See how quickly you can shift out of a negative space with something as simple as your thoughts. Once you get good at doing this, see how much more pleasurable your every moment will be.

67. Call a friend.

I have leaned on my friends my whole life. When I am going through a hard time, when I need a pick-me-up, when I want to laugh, when I want to express myself, when I want to just listen, or whatever, I call a friend. The moment I get on the phone, I immediately find myself in the moment of being myself and being a friend. There is nothing more gratifying.

How often do you call a friend when you want to talk, listen, or just be comforted by their friendship? The best part is when you call a friend and they say that they were just thinking about you or talking about you. It serves as a reminder of how connected we all are.

I've gotten to a point in my life in which I don't need to talk to my friends every day, every week, or even every month to know they are there for me no matter what. I just know that when I pick up the phone, whether it has been a week, month, year, or several years, I still know they are my friend. They remind me of how precious our moments are and can keep me grateful for living in the moment. Go ahead, pick up the phone, call a friend, and enjoy your moments together.

68. Be wrong some of the time.

Aim for success, not perfection.
Never give up your right to be wrong
because then you will lose the ability to learn new things
and move forward with your life.
~ David M. Burns

We like to be right, and while that's okay most of the time, it does have some negative fallout. We live in a society and world in which we are expected to be right all of the time. When I was in school, I was often afraid to raise my hand and ask questions because I didn't want to look like I didn't know anything. I have lived much of my life afraid to be wrong or do things the wrong way. I have held on to a need to look good and be right. What I am finding is that needing to be right has paralyzed me. It has held me back from expressing myself fully, from being myself, from trusting, and just from the experience of being wrong and learning from it.

I am beginning to let go of my expectations and the need to be right. Life is a lot more fun this way! I say things that I think and that are my truth even if they aren't the "right" answer. I listen better because I realize I don't need to be right. And really I have a lot more fun when I'm not so darn worried about being right all of the time! So cut loose, lighten up, relax, and get it wrong sometimes. You might find that you actually have a lot more fun and have a whole lot more going right for you in your life than when you had to be right all the time!

69. Complete the past.

In order to move forward in our lives, we must complete the past. What does this really mean? It means letting go of all the "baggage" we are holding onto. It means allowing ourselves to release our past and the things that are holding us back. It means finishing the things that we need to finish in order to feel ready to move forward.

I know for me, this is very true about my obligations. Before I can move forward in my life, I have to either complete the things that I have committed to or release myself from those commitments. I also know that I have been on a journey to let go of the wounds of my childhood. I have been working on forgiving my own imperfections and those of my family. I am finding that as I do that, I'm truly beginning to love them *and* myself unconditionally.

This is not an easy journey. Yet I am finding that the minute I handle whatever baggage I have my attention on and thereby complete the past, I can appreciate the present. What are the things in your life that you need to complete in order to truly be present?

70. LISTEN TO MUSIC.

The main thing is that we hear and
enjoy life's music everywhere.
~ THEODORE FONTANE

Many people die with their music still in them.
Why is this so? Too often it is because they are always getting
ready to live. Before they know it, time runs out.
~ OLIVER WENDELL HOLMES

Whenever I am in a funk, I listen to music and immediately I shift. It is amazing what music can do to bring about a smile on my face. The beat gets going, and my spirit rises. I wake up and come alive. I get in touch with my heart and soul, and I feel fully present in the world and all that life has to offer.

When I go through periods without music, life just seems to be hazy, dull, and definitely less vibrant. Often I don't even realize I have just gone through a period without music until I start listening again. The minute I do, I begin to feel the beat, rock and sway, bump and bounce, and live fully.

One time a friend came to visit and we went skiing. On the drive home, we started singing at the top of our lungs to Barry

White, Black Eyed Peas; you name it, we were singing it. How much fun and how alive were we? What more could you ask for in life? It is moments like these in which we can fully appreciate our aliveness. Listen to music and come alive!

71. GO CLIMB A TREE.

Always continue the climb.
It is possible for you to do whatever you choose,
if you first get to know who you are and are willing to work
with a power that is greater than ourselves to do it.
~ ELLA WHEELER WILCOX

Remember in childhood when climbing a tree was the most amazing thing to do? I do. I didn't climb a lot of trees; however, I remember the sense of self-satisfaction when I did. I felt like a little monkey who could just glide up the tree to that special spot. I remember perching on a tree with many branches and limbs. What a magical space. I could sit for hours and enjoy the day, watching people walk and cars whiz by. Even the bugs marching on entertained me as I would dangle from the branches and swing and play.

What is it about being a child that allows us to appreciate those moments? What is it about being an adult that often stops us cold from taking those risks, going on those expeditions, and following our joys? I am not really sure. For me, I think it is fear—fear of the unknown, fear of getting hurt, fear, fear, and more fear. I am not sure when I started to become so afraid. I just know that one day I was.

Recently I climbed a tree again, and I felt really free. Free of the fear, free of the worry, and just free to be me. I realized that finding moments like these where I can be free to breakthrough my fears and do something different, something fun, and something childlike, brings me back to my heart and brings me back to me. It reminds me of the moments that make up my life. If you get a chance, go climb a tree and see what it does for you.

72. Pass it on.

How many times in your life are you given a gift or an opportunity? How often does someone do something thoughtful that makes a difference in your day, week, month, year, or even your life? What if every time you were given one of these little gifts, you passed something on to someone else? Could you imagine living in a world where we were continually giving and receiving— in little ways or big ways? What would this planet look like?

Many of us have seen the movie *Pay it Forward*. If you haven't seen it, do so. It definitely gets at this concept of passing it on. If we are truly to live in the moment, imagine how much more fun it could be if every time we got something we passed something else like it along. We live in a world and society that is craving more relationships, more connectedness, and more giving. If we as adults could begin to take that on and model that behavior, imagine the difference it would make in our own lives, the lives of youth, and on this planet.

Next time you get a chance, pass along a little gift or a part of yourself—even something as simple as passing along a smile or making a phone call to let someone know that you were thinking about them. If you were wondering how to feel good living in the moment, imagine how good it feels to pass along a gift that just made you feel that special or loved.

73. LAUGH.

You grow up the day you have your first real laugh-at yourself.
~ ETHEL BARRYMORE

Laugh at yourself and at life. Not in the spirit of derision or whining self-pity, but as a remedy, a miracle drug, that will ease your pain, cure your depression, and help you to put in perspective that seemingly terrible defeat and worry with laughter at your predicaments, thus freeing your mind to think clearly toward the solution that is certain to come.
Never take yourself too seriously.
~ OG MANDINO

Laugh my friend, for laughter ignites a fire within the pit of your belly and awakens your being. Whatever it takes, find one minute every day to laugh *out loud*. My children do this so easily, so often. It is often contagious, laughter. I remember recently, as we were writing this book, I got a call. On the other end, my friend was stressed beyond measure over a lot of little things that built into one very overwhelming moment. Consciously listening to the multitude of issues that, at the time, seemed insurmountable to her, I burst into laughter.

She did the same. For a while we laughed. She felt better; I felt better, and suddenly the day felt lighter. Laughter elevates us out of the heaviness of life. When things seem overwhelming, laugh. There's no quicker way to get rid of the seriousness of whatever it is that's ailing you. Laughter puts things into perspective, and it immediately opens a space to be able to get in touch with what's valuable.

Laughter is a gift. It is place where we arrive that has no words, but it releases us, sets us free. Laughter's emotion is pure bliss. It opens our diaphragm and suddenly we are taking in full healing breaths of live energy. Enjoy laughing!

74. Hold yourself capable.

For much of my life, I haven't held myself capable. That is, I haven't trusted myself to handle whatever comes my way. When I don't hold myself capable, I don't hold others capable either.

Often in our society, we don't hold the people we love and care about capable because we want to protect them from pain. We don't want them to get hurt, be disappointed, or make mistakes. When others don't hold us capable, we begin to doubt ourselves. We stop trusting ourselves and believing in all that we are capable of.

This has been true in my own life. I have not fully trusted myself to make choices. I have not held myself capable, so I have lived much of my life in fear and playing it safe. I am just now beginning to hold myself capable and as a result, I'm more willing to put myself out there. I am able to be true to who I am as I know the gifts that I have to offer the world.

Trust yourself and hold yourself and others capable of all that you are. While it might be a little uncomfortable, you may begin to see how much more you can truly accomplish when you do.

75. SUFFERING IS OPTIONAL.

I cannot believe that the inscrutable universe turns
on an axis of suffering; surely the strange beauty of the
world must somewhere rest on pure joy.

~ LOUISE BOGAN

How true is this statement: "suffering is optional"? I mean seriously, how often do we make our lives so much more difficult than we have to? It can be something as small as beating ourselves up when we haven't done something we said we would or getting mad when people don't call us back or when we do something and the result isn't what we expected or hoped for. I know for me, I often choose to make life a lot more difficult and to suffer through it more than enjoying it.

Don't get me wrong. There is a lot of wrong being done around the world that results in too much pain or suffering. However, how often do we choose to suffer over things that really aren't worth suffering over? How often do we choose to get buried in overwhelm or get caught up in what is wrong, rather than enjoying what we do have and focusing on that a little more every day?

I learned that life is hard, *"La vita e dura,"* as the Italians say. For a long time I believed that, and I lived my life that way, making everything more difficult than it had to be. Somewhere along the line I realized it wasn't working for me, and I was creating much of my own suffering.

In my journey, I became aware that it was my choice to suffer or not. So now I like to live more by the expression, "Life is good." I even like to think that life is *great*! Try it on for size. See what life can be like if you recognize suffering is optional and that you can choose to live in happiness rather than suffering!

76. Be true to yourself.

*Always be a first-rate version of yourself, instead of
a second rate version of somebody else.*

~ Judy Garland

Sometimes we forget to be true to ourselves. We can focus on everything that we are not and forget all that we are. Rather than trying to be like everyone else or to live up to what other people expect of us, we need to remember that we are unique. Really, how boring would the world be if we were all the same?

Unfortunately, too much of our lives are spent trying to fit in. How much happier would we each be if we could fully be who we are? How much more special would our moments in life be if we were each being true to ourselves and could appreciate each other for who we really are?

I know in my life this has been a tough one for me. When I have asked myself the question, "am I true to myself all hours of the day?" I haven't always answered yes. In fact, I find many times throughout the day that I am not fully being true to myself, that I show up part of the way, yet hold back parts of me because of my fear of what others think. Sometimes when I'm with my family or with my clients, I won't reveal *all* of me because I don't want to feel disapproval.

What if we could begin to let go of these fears and see this from a different perspective? What would life be like if we could spend more of our lives being our authentic selves? I have decided that I am going to show up fully as who I am, and if I am rejected or disapproved of, it is their loss, not mine.

As I go through the journey to appreciate each and every moment in my life, I am finding that I am beginning to let go of some of the need to be what others think I should be and truer to who my heart and soul tells me I am. This is what life is about. Remember to let your true self out. You might be surprised how much easier it gets every day, and you might be amazed at how much better every moment becomes!

77. Make a choice, take action, and move forward.

Just because we cannot see clearly the end of the road, that is no reason for not setting out on the essential journey.
~ John F. Kennedy

Just begin by taking one step or doing one thing.
~ Barbara DeAngelis

Often we get stuck at a crossroads when we have a decision to make. We may be paralyzed by fear or afraid of making the wrong choice. We may have too few options or even too many, but none of them are very good. Whatever the case may be, making a choice, taking action, and moving forward is always better than being stuck in the same place for too long.

I often forget that when I get stuck. I get so caught up in where I'm at, I don't believe I can keep moving forward. I focus on where I am at rather than where I am going. Sometimes I just have to reflect for a moment and then take the next leap forward.

So the next time you get stuck, give yourself a moment to reflect and then trust your intuition, make a choice and just take the next right step. Generally, there are two possibilities once you make the choice; you will either succeed or fail. If you fail, rather than seeing it as a negative, take it as an opportunity to say that you risked, that you attempted something different, and while it didn't turn out as planned, you learned from it. Really in the end, nothing is worse than being stuck where you were. So go for it, live a little!

78. Write it down.

So many times I have been paralyzed by my thoughts. At any given moment, I may have so many thoughts in my head that I become overwhelmed and don't know where to start or which way to turn. When I get to that point, I find that if I stop for a moment and write down what's in my head, it helps release the thoughts that are swirling around. It doesn't matter what I write them on—the back of an envelope, a scrap piece of paper, even a register receipt. This is different from journaling. This is simply writing down my thoughts, and it has a marvelous effect. It clears a space for me to move from thought to action.

Clearing the clutter from my head by putting it on paper calms my mind and lowers my anxiety level. It serves as a mechanism to make some space in my brain for new thoughts instead of obsessing on old thoughts. It enables me to see the thoughts that were in my head and to move on. Often I find that, until I write things down, I get stuck in the "analysis paralysis" of whatever is in my head. The next time you are caught in overload or overwhelm, write it down and see if it helps you to shift and move on.

79. Putter around.

Puttering is really a time to be alone, to dream and
to get in touch with yourself... To putter is to discover.

~ Alexandra Stoddard

When did I stop puttering around? I distinctly remember moments in middle school, high school, and even college when I used to putter around, but at some point, that all stopped. I am not sure why. I was recently reminded that everything I do in life doesn't have to be out of obligation. Everything doesn't have to be practical, but somehow as I have gotten older this has become more and more the case. It was the message I got as a child—duty and responsibility—and so I became diligent, hard working, and extremely productive. But I stopped having fun, stopped doing things that needed no justification other than just because I felt like it.

That is what puttering around is about. Setting about without a direction, without a purpose, and just leaving time to be, wander, and discover as you go. It is funny how long I have avoided puttering and as such I have avoided facing myself, facing my dreams, and learning who I am. As I begin to allow more time to myself to putter, explore, dream, and discover, I find I am being freed of the need to succeed and do. Puttering is quite liberating. Try it sometime and see!

80. HAVE AN ICE-CREAM CONE
WITH A FRIEND.

My advice to you is not to inquire why or whither,
but just enjoy your ice-cream while it's on your plate—
that's my philosophy.
- THORNTON WILDER

"I screama, you screama, we all screama for ice-cream-a." Every time I think of ice cream, I think of Roberto Benigni in the movie *Down By Law*. It is a tremendous scene in which the Italian actor is in jail and circles around the jail cell with his cell mates, singing this tune, getting louder and louder at every pass.

That is the way I feel about ice cream! I love ice cream—every kind and particularly gelato! So many memories of my best moments in life involve ice cream, especially as a kid. Whether it was going to Baskin Robbins for green-mint-chocolate-chip ice cream or eating ice cream almost religiously every Friday night in high school with my friends Robin and Katie, the memories are always happy ones.

In Italy, going to a "bar" isn't just about drinking alcohol. It serves a combination of coffee, ice cream, and liquor; it is the cornerstone of their culture. The whole family goes. Three generations—kids, parents, and grandparents—often sit together enjoying the evening, and my family was no different. I would always get the same flavors: *nocciola*, *nutella*, and *baccio* gelato "*con panna*" (with whipped cream). Oh the memories and smiles that went along with that ice cream.

In college, I befriended a homeless man whom I would take out for an ice-cream cone. We would talk to about his life and how he ended up homeless. I was amazed at the stories and wondered how it was possible for this man to live on the street in Madison, Wisconsin through the cold harsh winters and survive. Yet he lived to tell the stories and share an ice-cream cone with a naïve college girl who was curious about life and looking for answers. Those were pretty powerful moments and pretty special ice-cream cones.

When I think of ice cream, I immediately smile—not just because I love ice cream, but because I love the moments in my life I can remember that are connected with ice cream.

When was the last time you went out and enjoyed an ice-cream cone with a friend? What are you waiting for? You might just have some pretty special moments that stay with you for the rest of your life!

81. Go to your favorite place.

Where is your favorite place? We all have a place in this world that refreshes, revitalizes, and fulfills us. But how often do we go there? Because favorite places are sometimes hard to get to, sometimes it's possible to conjure up the peace and calmness a favorite place brings just by visiting it in our minds. But how often do we even do that?

My favorite place is anywhere near water. I have only begun to realize how much I love the water. When I was growing up, I was blessed with being able to spend many of my summers at our family beach home in Italy. Perhaps I love water because of all the pleasant memories associated with that beach house. No matter how long we had been gone, when my brother and I arrived at the beach, we would be treated as if we were coming home. We'd tell stories and exchange gifts and despite a year or two's absence, it was as though no time had passed at all. We would play volleyball, soccer, or paddle ball on the beach and build the best sand castles and tracks for marble races. I would do dozens of back handsprings in a row—all day long. We would body surf, row out into the sea on our "*patiné*" (little wood row boats) and play in the sea.

To me, water represents the pure joy and happiness of being in the moment. Today every time I am near water, all of those feelings return. Now I am learning that when I am not near water, I can re-create that in my mind, and it is as if I am there.

When was the last time you visited your favorite place—either for real or in your mind? Your body doesn't know the difference between the reality and the vision in your mind. So don't use the fact that your favorite place isn't near you as an excuse not to go there. Take some time whenever you can, whether in person or otherwise, to be in your favorite place and savor the moment.

82. Make mistakes.

*The greatest mistake you can make in life is
to be continually fearing you will make one.*
~ Elbert Hubbard

*Freedom is not worth having if it does not include
the freedom to make mistakes.*
~ Mahatma Gandhi

Wow! If it were not for all the mistakes I've made, I certainly would not be where I am today. The successes, the pleasures, and the gifts of love and joy in my life are the absolute result of making mistake after mistake—and learning something. This was not always the case.

Making mistakes growing up was nothing short of a disaster, at least to my sense of self. I felt compelled to compare myself to everyone, always ending up last. The concept of not being "enough" became a big part of my story because it was the way I measured myself. Over years of playing this game, my self-esteem hit bottom.

However, one of the highlights of my life's journey has been in finding the gift in making mistakes. Of course I don't make mistakes on purpose, but they happen as I put myself out there and try new things. Mistakes have become opportunities to learn more about some situation or my response to a situation. Mistakes are often just what I need to push me in a new direction, or question the reason I've made the choice that has placed me in the situation I happen to be in at any given moment. And most of all, mistakes are the reason I succeed. My mistakes contribute to making me stronger, wiser, and often much more aware.

Making mistakes is not scary; they are a part of life that can be gifts that allow new choices to be made, opening the door for new opportunities and successes. I am grateful for all the opportunities I've had to make a mistake because I know it is how I've grown.

83. Spend time with seniors.

In Italy, spending time with seniors is part of the culture. Unlike in American society in which there is a distinct separation of seniors, I was raised in environments where seniors were a natural part and centerpiece of the community. As I said in the ice-cream section, we would go to the "bar", an Italian café where all the generations would often come together—"*i Nonni*" (the grandparents) with parents and children. The *Nonni* would be drinking their café; the parents, a liqueur; and the children would eat a gelato. Three generations would sit together, share, and be together. Seniors were looked at with respect and looked to for their wisdom, experience, and life stories. They were honored.

The way we treat seniors in the U.S. has been very hard for me to deal with. There is such a separation as seniors are not respected and revered in the same way as they are in Italian culture. They almost seem as if they are a burden on society. How did that happen? We have disconnected from the very people from whom we could learn so much. How will we truly learn not to make the same mistakes we have made in history if we aren't willing to spend time with our seniors to listen and learn from them?

Go spend some time with a senior. Whether it is one of your own relatives or someone in a home, it doesn't matter. By visiting them, you could brighten their day and also learn a lot yourself. You might be surprised at the mutual joy you could bring to each other by sharing those moments together.

84. Go ride a bike.

As you can probably already tell, I love my bike. Before I sat down to write this, I went for a bike ride. It was a good reminder of what life is about, taking breaks and living in the moment. It is funny how wrapped up I can get in life, yet my most amazing and creative moments come when I let go and allow myself to relax and reconnect with divine inspiration.

Riding a bike is extra special for me, and some of my fondest memories come from being on my bike. I can even remember back when I was a little girl and my father taught me to ride. One of my happiest memories is of him running behind me, holding on to the back of the seat. I felt so safe and secure knowing that he was there. I was so excited. I yelled something back to my daddy, only to realize that he let go. As the realization hit, I lost all my confidence and immediately fell over. Yet the moment will be with me forever.

As an adult I have many wonderful bike-riding memories. I even named my bike, Happy, or "*Epi*" as the Italians would pronounce it. One of the most special moments was when I raced Ironman, Austria. It was such an amazing day. I kept smiling, waving to all the fans, and saying hello to everyone I passed or whoever passed me. I was just happy to be alive and riding my bike. When

I finished the race, a fan came up to me and told me that I had the biggest smile on my face of anyone racing. It was true. It was probably one of the happiest days of my life.

It is the little things in life that make it so special. Get out, ride a bike, and see what memories return or what new memories you may create.

85. GIVE YOURSELF A GIFT.

We must possess love before we can give.

~ MOTHER TERESA

How often do we give ourselves a gift? I find it very easy to give to others, so much so that I often give to others before I would ever consider giving to myself. I give my time to others. I give money to others. I give little thoughtful gifts. And yet when it comes to me, I rarely give myself a gift. As I have started to truly love and value myself, I have begun to give myself more gifts. Sometimes they are material gifts, but other times they are less concrete gifts like time to myself, being gentle with myself, taking care of myself, or having fun.

It doesn't matter exactly what the gift looks like as long as you are giving to yourself on a regular basis. If we value ourselves and love ourselves, it becomes more possible to love and give more to others.

86. Be still.

Do you have the patience to wait until your mud settles
and the water is clear? Can you remain unmoving
until the right action arises by itself?

~ Lao Tsu

How many of us find ourselves doing two, three, even four tasks all at once? I remember one time I was watching television, which I rarely do, and I found myself writing thank-you cards and talking on the phone at the same time. When I finished all of my tasks and turned off the television, I remember thinking to myself, how often is it that I just focus on one thing at a time, rather than multi-tasking? Then the question popped into my head: how often do I actually just sit still and be? I remember being almost haunted by that question. I didn't really even know what "being still" meant.

So occasionally now and again, I set aside some time to just be still. The first few times I tried it, I literally didn't know what to do with myself. Yet over time, I am beginning to really enjoy those moments. They may be few and far between, yet every time I sit down to just be still, whether it is for ten minutes or a few hours, I find myself breathing, relaxing, and just being grounded and centered with myself. It is quite freeing to know that I can just be and don't have to run off somewhere and do something. It also is amazing what kind of things come to me in those moments, the clarity, the creativity, and the vision. Try being still sometime and see what happens in your universe.

87. Practice patience.

He that can have patience, can have what he will.
~ Benjamin Franklin

I was taught impatience by society around me. Every day our world gets a little bit more hectic, busy, and full of things to do. Every new invention makes it more convenient to keep up with the fast pace of life. We have packaged foods, fast foods, and gadgets to help us keep up or just get by. But we are not being taught patience; we are being taught to hurry up and to expect others to speed up as well.

Whatever it takes, and despite all we are taught, remembering to practice patience allows us to live more in harmony and in less of a rush. Being patient allows us to let go of some of our expectations of ourselves and others and to be free to live more in the moment.

88. LOVE YOURSELF

FOR ALL THAT YOU ARE.

Until you make peace with who you are,
you'll never be content with what you have.
~ DORIS MORTMAN

I have spent so much of my life accomplishing amazing things. Yet I never give myself any credit for those things. Instead, I am finding that I have often focused on the one little thing that I didn't accomplish or didn't get quite right rather than the fifty things I did amazingly well. It is funny how that is. When I was growing up in school, I was a really good student. Yet when I got something wrong, that was often what was pointed out and so that was what I focused on. If I had a test and got ninety-nine out of one hundred right, it was the one wrong that had a big red *X* and was the focus.

Today I am finding this is still often the case. Recently I had a great weekend, and I achieved a bunch of goals I had set and had dreamed about for a long time. Yet when the weekend was over, I focused on the one or two things that I had not done very well, and I was literally exhausted, overwhelmed, and upset with myself. When I took a minute to get some perspective, I realized that I was doing this yet again. It hit me really hard. I realized that it is and has always been a choice for me to focus on what I have not accomplished or what I am not, rather than celebrating all that I do accomplish and what an amazing woman I am. I also became aware that if I focus on what I am not doing, then I will never love myself or appreciate all that I do accomplish every day in my life.

If this resonates with you, think about it and remember to be gentle with yourself. Focus on and remind yourself of all that you have accomplished. Even if you have only accomplished one thing that day, focus on that instead of all of the things you didn't accomplish. You may find by ending your day focusing on the one or many positive things you did that day, it becomes easier every day to focus on that instead of the thing or things you didn't do so well. Little by little, these positive messages might start sinking in so that one day you might wake up and truly love yourself for all that you are and all that you have become!

89. SPEAK YOUR TRUTH.

*The moment we begin to fear the opinions of others and
hesitate to tell the truth that is in us, and from motives of policy
are silent when we should speak, the divine floods of light and
life no longer flow into our souls.*

~ ELIZABETH CADY STANTON

Speak your truth even if it is going to ruffle some feathers. This goes along "be true to yourself," for when you are being your true self, it is much easier to speak what you know is true.

For as long as I can remember, I have been afraid to speak my truth. When situations come up that require me to speak my truth and share from within, I often get choked up or I find myself holding my truths back.

I think this is a result of not speaking my truth as a child. I was often expected to appear a certain way. When I did speak my truth, when I was being my true self, I was often told to stop dreaming and to plant my feet back on the ground instead of floating in the clouds. I interpreted that as needing to be someone different than who I really was in order to get by or succeed. As a result, I began to quiet my truth within. In fact, it got to the point that not only did I shut down my truth, I didn't even know what my own truth was. I have begun to break through much of that and am beginning to truly know myself and my inner truths. I am learning that no longer do I have to dim my inner light and gifts, nor do I have to hold back my inner truths.

Whatever the case may be, there is nothing more important than speaking up and sharing your truth. This is the starting place to know yourself, to love yourself, trust, and believe in yourself. As a result, you will find you love others more easily. It is the foundation to being able to live freely and fully and to live every day in the moment with inner peace and joy.

90. BELIEVE IN HUMANITY.

An individual has not started living until he can rise above
the narrow confines of his individualistic concerns
to the broader concerns of all humanity.
~ MARTIN LUTHER KING, JR.

I grew up in a very small town. I recall vividly the moment I connected with the largeness of humanity; it was the night my grandmother woke me to watch the astronauts walk on the moon. On a black-and- white television, I watched in awe as I shared the wonder of Neil Armstrong walking on the moon. The way my grandmother explained the vastness of space and the smallness of our planet was beautiful, and I realized the beauty came from my believing in the goodness and the connectedness of humanity.

I have spent my life traveling, knowing I will touch all the corners of the world, touch all of humanity. Once, as I was traveling though Asia, I was picked up by a small local van on a remote island in Indonesia. I always make it a point to take local public transportation. Happy to have a ride, I realized we started traveling in the opposite direction from where I wanted to go. We got way off the beaten path, as it were, but I trusted that my fellow traveling companions had my best interests at heart. When we stopped, everyone got off and started preparing a healing ceremony for a young child. I was actually an integral part of the ceremony as I was asked to hold the child.

Afterwards, during the meal, I asked someone why I was brought to this place. This person told me that they needed my energy to complete the healing. This was amazing. My grandmother was a healer, as I have said, but for a long time I refused to accept the reality of that. This was the first time I understood the incredible power in healing, and I was awed at the enormous power of connection that came from this moment.

If we're too busy judging what people offer in our lives instead of just believing in their goodness, we completely miss out on the opportunity to connect, to become part of the thread of humanity.

We need to believe in the goodness of each individual person before it's even possible to begin to connect. And even more important, we have to believe in our own goodness first, believe that we have something to contribute. Then we can reach out and believe in others, and only then will we connect with our fellow brothers and sisters.

Our contribution to humanity comes in many ways, is shared in many ways, and reaches across all boundaries. Believe in yourself, in humankind, and be open to the connection that comes with belief.

91. Open your presents slowly.

Each day comes bearing its gifts. Untie the ribbons.
~ Ann Ruth Schabacher

I grew up celebrating both Chanukah and Christmas as a child. What a treat! I got presents for Chanukah and then would also get a mass of presents on Christmas day! Back then I would tear through them. Within a matter of minutes, all of the wrapping would be in a pile in the middle of the room, all the presents spread out around the room, and I would either be playing with or wearing my favorite.

Today, I have learned to open my presents slowly. I don't get as many presents as when I was a child, yet I definitely have learned to appreciate them more and treasure the moment of actually opening the gift. I am now able to relish in the thoughtfulness of the giver and appreciate the act of giving. I am more open to truly receiving the gift. I open the card slowly and read the words and take them in fully. I then untie the ribbons slowly, spending time to enjoy the wrapping and the care with which the gift was wrapped. Once I've unwrapped the present, I spend a long moment with whomever gave it to me—even if it is myself—expressing my gratitude for this amazing gift.

I am finding more and more how much I can appreciate the small gifts, even when it is little more than a thought. I treasure the fact that someone thought of me enough to give me a present. The next time you get a present, really take the time to open it slowly and be in the moment of giving!

92. WITNESS THE BIRTH OF A BABY.

A miracle cannot prove what is impossible,
it is useful only to confirm what is possible...

~ MAIMONIDES

There are some experiences that are difficult to convey; seeing the birth of a baby is one of them. It is a miracle that has moved me like no other. I have given birth. I have watched babies being born, and it is all pure bliss. It is definitely at the top of my "most joyful moments" list.

Three times I have been given the gift of allowing life into the world through me. Each experience, and each child, has been completely different. Birth is a miracle that has expanded my ability to believe in the impossible. It has persuaded me to believe in miracles. If out of nothing, a tiny microscopic cell can become the physical manifestation of a human being, what else is possible? I am awed by the absolute magnificence of life.

Of all the human experiences, there is a power and magic in the experience of birth that is indescribable, unpredictable, and life-inspiring. Have an experience with birth, and if you can, have several. Your heart will open wide. If you can hold the memory of the magic and miracle of birth, then you will hold the true gift for yourself—that of opening your heart to yourself and others.

93. Shop for a treasure.

*There is a vitality, a life-force, an energy, a quickening that is
translated through you into action and because there is
only one of you in all of time, this expression is unique.
And if you block it, it will never exist
through any other medium and be lost.*

~ Martha Graham

Flea markets evoke interesting responses, and for me, they represent a true treasure hunt. My friend and jewelry artist mentor, Lynne Merchant, took me to a flea market in Paris. I was mesmerized by all the stuff, most of it old, dusty, and seemingly questionable in its use. That is until I surrendered to a new way of looking at junk. Hidden in boxes and corners or sometimes in piles are treasures. It takes time and patience to find them, but oh the joy when you do. At this particular Parisian market, I thought I had looked through everything in a certain box, and there at the very bottom, I picked up a chain. It revealed itself to be an antique pocket watch fob. Not certain what I could create out of it, Lynne suggested I fashion it into a necklace by adding some additional hand-made chain. This sounded like a great idea.

I stood in front of a mirror with my final creation around my neck. Amazed at the beauty of my new necklace, I realized I too am like the watch fob. If I am willing to take the time to create something beautiful from what is, I too can transform myself, my life, and my dreams. Treasures are found in unpredictable places. Often when we least expect to find a treasure, it appears. Look inside yourself; dust off the old no longer usable or desired corners of darkness. Forgive yourself, love yourself, and reveal your treasures.

94. Stop trying so hard.

Don't make an effort because the best things happen
when you least expect them.

~ Unknown

"Try easy" instead of trying so hard! It is when I am willing to surrender that my life flows. It is easy to say or think about "trying easy," yet actually doing it can be a gigantic struggle.

I find this struggle in my life most often occurs when I fall into a controlling attitude. When I come from a place of wanting to control the conversation or the situation, I feel stressed and uncomfortable. My body becomes tight and my breathing slows, almost stopping. I find that all of my energy shifts the moment I let go and "try easy." When I send love and understanding to the person I feel I am in a struggle with as opposed to wanting to control them, it becomes easy.

Sometimes getting to the point of realizing I am in a place of wanting to control is tough because the control factor is an unconscious action for me. However, my body is my best teacher. The more I stop and listen to myself and feel what's happening in my body, the sooner I am able to let go. Stop trying so hard and "try easy!" You will breathe easier and feel better.

195

95. Feel the rain on your skin.

Feel the rain on your skin; no one else can feel it for you,
only you can let it in, no one else,
no one else can speak the words on your lips.

~ Natasha Bedingfield

I recently heard this quote in a song, and it took me back to my adolescence. I remember as a teenager, I would go out with my friends in spring and summer during the rain. We would take our shoes off and run around in the rain, stomp in puddles, and feel the rain on our skin. I felt so alive, so unafraid and carefree, so happy.

As I sit here and write about those moments, I can even remember the smell of the rain hitting the asphalt. Ahhhhh, there is nothing like the smell of the earth cooling down on a hot and humid Philadelphia- summer day. I remember thinking, as I splashed through puddles, that I was rebellious because I wasn't wearing shoes and was completely disregarding the rules. So much of the time, I was constrained by what people thought about me, what I should be doing, or how I should act. But with the rain on my skin, I was free. I didn't care what people thought so much, and in those moments, I felt as though I didn't have a care in the world. I didn't have to get everything right or be something that someone else wanted me to be. In those moments playing in the rain, I could fully be who I was.

How often do we get moments like these in our lives? I know for me, I didn't have many until recently, or if I did, I didn't recognize and enjoy these moments too often. Through writing this book, I am finding more and more moments like these every day. It is these moments that life is really about! Get out there and feel the rain on your skin, splash around in the puddles, and remember what it was like to be a rebellious teenager. Enjoy all that is your life—*now*!

96. Let your inner light

shine bright.

*Learn the craft of knowing how to open your heart and to turn
on your creativity. There's a light inside of you.*

~ Judith Jamison

I feel as though much of my life I have been asked to dim my
inner lights. It reminds me of the story of Rudolph the Red-nosed
Reindeer. You know how it goes. Rudolf has a red nose, the other
reindeers laugh and don't let Rudolf play in their reindeer games,
until one day they see the value in that shiny nose, and they let
Rudolf lead the sleigh.

As I have gotten older and come into my own, I realize that this
is a very familiar experience for me. While my nose isn't shiny, my
inner soul and energy sure shine really bright!

I am creative, energetic, and full of exciting ideas and dreams.
Often in my life, I have found that this enthusiasm for life has
scared or threatened people and has often resulted in me being
misunderstood, pushed to the side, or told to "back off" a little bit.
It has even scared me at times. Once, when I was frustrated with
some of my relationships, I had a friend tell me that with some

people I was just "too intense." At the time, my response was to lessen my intensity.

I am starting to understand that I don't have to dim my lights because of my own fears or those of others. I can truly let my inner light shine bright. I can be true to who I am, and when I do, I can then trust that everything will work out. Today let your inner light shine bright and see how good it feels!

97. LISTEN TO YOUR INTUITION.

Intuition is a spiritual faculty, and does not explain,
but simply points the way.
~ FLORENCE SCOVEL SHINN

Buddha left a road map, Jesus left a road map,
Krishna left a road map, Rand McNally left a road map.
But you still have to travel the road yourself...
~ STEPHEN LEVINE

When I was a young girl, my mother announced one summer that I would be spending the summer in Miami with my "Mother Pilar" (my father's mother). Having never spent much time with "Mother Pilar," I was very excited. I was especially excited about flying on an airplane to get there. With my packed bags, off to the airport we went. But as soon as it was time for me to board the airplane, I stopped, looked at my mother and the flight attendant and said, "NO, I'm not getting on the plane." I started to cry as my mother insisted I get aboard. I threw a fit. I stomped my feet and absolutely refused. The flight attendant was no longer willing to have me aboard either. I remember saying to my mother, "I'll go tomorrow, but I am *not* getting on *that plane today.*" My mother was less than pleased with me, until the news report later that day. It featured the story of a flight hijacked to Cuba. It was the flight I was scheduled to take...

Years have passed since that day. I did go visit my "Mother Pilar" the next week, and I've flown many times since. And there have been times when I have allowed my intuition to be overridden by my logic. In the end, my intuition is *always* right. The more I am willing to listen to my still, knowing inner voice, the more smoothly my life flows. Listen to and trust your intuition.

98. Go sit with a cat.

Yes it really says that. One night I called my friend in a frenzy. My exact words were, "I am *freaking out.*" When I said that, she just started laughing at me. Instead of getting mad that she wasn't being sympathetic, I just started laughing in response. It was an immediate switch for me, and it allowed me to hear her advice. As we began talking, she said, "Go sit with a cat." I nearly hung up the phone I was laughing so hard. Yet when she explained to me what she was talking about, I realized she was serious. What she meant was for me to go find a cuddly cat to sit quietly with so that I could be comforted by it, calmed by it, or whatever I needed at that moment. (If you aren't a cat person any cuddly animal works fine.)

It seemed pretty ridiculous at the time, and still does, yet it made me smile and laugh. I also realized as I sat with a cat that that there is nothing better to bring me back to *now* than being calmed down with the love of an animal.

99. TAKE RISKS.

Only those who will risk going too far
can possibly find out how far one can go.
~ T.S. ELIOT

I am a risk taker. It is one of my qualities I value most—most of the time. I don't even notice that I take risks until I am with someone who is risk adverse.

Risk is another way of looking at life. Risk is like the ripe shiny apples I would climb the tree for as a young girl. Sometimes, I skinned my knee on the way up the tree. Often I would slip and even fall. However, the juicy, fresh taste of a ripe apple, the ones that were always as high as I could reach, was a reward well worth the risk.

All along we've talked about how living in the moment involves various forms of risk, but here I want to address one of the greatest risks I take daily. It is the risk I take when I choose my heart over my head, when I choose yang over yin, intuitive energy over rational energy.

I think of it as the plague of our Western existence. We've been taught always to go with the rational, symbolically represented as the male energy of the earth and sun as opposed to the symbolically female energy of water and the moon. However, life always represents a choice, and we can either move forward and experience life or move back into the safety of what's known. Everyday, I risk making a conscious choice to move from a space of thinking, the space of logic and rational thinking, to allowing myself to feel. And I have found that risking existence in the realm of the irrational, of intuition, of love, is the most rewarding, the most pure. Love and feelings are easily talked about and justified, but how often are we willing to risk living from our heart and sharing our feelings?

100. LIVE IN ABUNDANCE.

There is enough in the world for everyone's need;
there is not enough for everyone's greed...

~ MAHATMA GANDHI

When you realize there is nothing lacking,
the whole world belongs to you...

~ LAO TSU

Growing up I was exposed to extremes. I spent my early childhood being given abundant amounts of love and so I was able to love abundantly back. However, once I was removed from the safe cocoon that Mammy and the farm represented, all that changed. My adolescence was wrought with scarcity. My parents struggled to provide food, clothing, and even shelter. I recall often feeling scared when my parents were fearful of how we would eat, and so I was reprogrammed to think and believe in scarcity.

Then when I went to live with my aunt and uncle, a light turned on; I remembered the earlier option of abundance. While my aunt and uncle didn't have much in the way of material goods, they did have an abundance of love, and they also voiced their gratitude for what they did have everyday. With them, I learned that abundance and gratitude are inextricable.

I am now so grateful for everything that I have! I also know that when you believe in abundance, you can then live in abundance, *and* you can only keep abundance flowing if you are always grateful for what comes to you.

It is by living in a state of gratitude that abundance flows into my life. Gratitude is pure love, the place I find the greatest connection to my God or Source. An abundance of health, wealth, and happiness is ours for the taking if we live with gratitude. Reflecting back on my years spent with my parents, I realize the real lack in their lives came from a lack of love and gratitude. Abundance follows gratitude, so believe in abundance, live in gratitude, and watch the world respond!

101. Remember we are human beings not human doings.

Often people attempt to live their lives backwards:
they try to have more things, or more money, in order to
do more of what they want so that they will be happier.
The way it actually works is the reverse. You must first
be who you really are, then do what you need to do,
in order to have what you want.

~ Margaret Young

Need we say more? Seriously though! Sometimes it is hard to remember that we are human beings any more. We are constantly bombarded with everything to keep us moving faster, doing more, and doing it quicker. Some days I even wonder to myself, what does "to be" mean?

What does it mean to be a human being any more when all I ever do is *do*! I have moments of real sadness because my most amazing moments in life are being—being human! The moments that always stick with me are those when I am connecting with other human beings, and it reminds me of my aliveness. The moments I will always remember are those when I am being the most human. I remember most the moments when I …

Connect with people

Am compassionate

Work with youth and communities in need

Visit old friends and relatives

Act like a goofball

Meet someone new for the first time.

These are the moments I remember. I rarely remember moments when I am doing—even when I have done amazing things. I often have skipped by even the most outrageous achievements in a hurry to move on to the next one. So what it really boils down to is appreciating all that we are as human beings and not all that we do, plain and simple.

I meditate daily. This simple time of silence provides the space for me to connect to my beingness. My father taught me how to meditate, but after leaving home, there were several years when I deviated from my meditation practice. I did a lot during those years. I accomplished a lot, and I fortunately found a teacher who reintroduced me to the practice of meditation. As I began to meditate I found comfort again in my beingness.

As I take time to be still and listen, I have come to know that I am a being, an energy, and I have a physical body. And the synergy of the two together becomes my human being.

I can accomplish so much more when I am in this state of knowing I am a human being. It is when I am being that I am connected to my purpose, my vision, and my dreams. But I also know that without my body, my spirit would not have the power to take action and to create amazing gifts in our world. I've become aware of the fantastic power we have to change the world, to shift the direction of our world for good, when we align as beings expressing our beingness.

Giving is the expression of my beingness in the world. As we find our beingness, it becomes easier to let go of doing without purpose and passion. When we are being light and love, everything we need and all the right people show up in our lives and fly with us. Find your beingness, celebrate your beingness, and soar.

Final Thoughts I

Grace, Gratitude, and Giving

~ CYNTHIA ALIZA BLAKE

In the pages of this book, something has happened; a chapter of my life has emerged. It looks vaguely as I imagined it to be. I am reminded of a story that was told to me while I back-packed through Bali many years ago. Following a lightning storm, which left two people dead, I realized I'd left my Lonely Planet guide book in a local van I had taken a ride with. I thought I had lost my bible, for this was the book that told me how to navigate through Asia—what to see, where to go for food and lodging, that sort of thing.

As I explained my predicament to the young men who managed the place where I was staying, they told me about two people who had been killed by lightning earlier in the day. I suddenly realized how unimportant my travel book was. I offered my condolences, only to be awakened by the response, which I have never forgotten. One of the men said, "The Gods willed it." Wow, I was speechless, but then they said something else that really blew me away. These young men, who were very intuitive, simply said to me, "Do not worry. Your book will return if that is what is best for you. It must be what is in your purpose; then it will come back." I went off to my tiny hut for the evening, grateful for the break in rain that was a welcomed part of my day during the rainy season in Southeast Asia. As I journaled this story in the silence of the night, I pondered my purpose and how something so seemingly small as a travel book could be part of it.

That night I dreamt of a world of beauty and peace. I woke to find my Lonely Planet travel book outside my hut near the gratitude offering that is made every morning by the Hindu people. I was at first surprised, but I quickly became excited and ultimately grateful. I understood that my journey through the rest of this great region of the world was about letting go and experiencing life in all the moments that it presents itself.

These are the gifts that allow the unfolding of who we are, and more important, I realized the connection to giving. Throughout my journey in the Indonesian Islands, I was provided for without question or expectation, and I found that I had to accept all that was given to me with grace. I understood intrinsically that grace is the willingness to accept our gifts instead of fighting them or refusing them because we feel we don't deserve them.

This incident happened early on in my back-packing trip, and by losing and then being given my Lonely Planet travel book back, I knew that my gift was fully understanding what it means to live in the present and be grateful for all the new experiences that came my way. And it didn't have to always be the "big stuff." The events of everyday became inherent gifts as they were daily explorations of my own connection to life and the universe around me.

As I journeyed on, I came to an island at the far reaches of Indonesia. It's called Bunaken Island, and it's reached only by a small boat. The island is unusual in that it has both a Muslim and a Hindu village. I unknowingly took a ride on the boat that would take me to the Muslim village. I was greeted by a beautiful family and taken to their home where I was given the children's room to lay my head. The home was beautifully cared for. The floors of dirt were cool and welcoming. Outside a hole in the ground served to keep their food cool and away from the animals.

The entire village came to see the Westerner. The children sat on my lap, touched my hair, and shared their language with me. They brought flowers and food to share. One night I was awakened by pounding and hammering. The neighbor next to us had passed in the night and the entire village was building a casket. As I helped, I was so touched by the giving that I had experienced, in the short time I had been on the island.

As I watched the community giving and sharing in celebrating the life of one of its members, I was again reminded of the power of giving. No matter where I found myself, on this island and elsewhere through Asia, I was always given a place to stay; I was always offered food, and I was continually given the chance to experience being in other people's lives by being asked to celebrate life's passages—births, deaths, and important moments in between. From this, I could truly comprehend what I had learned as a child. I had lived my life from a giving space, but this helped me to see that when you give in abundance you receive in abundance.

Ultimately, my journey back-packing through Asia was a turning point in my life because it was the point at which I realized I was here to empower others to find and live their greatness through an abundance of giving.

These lessons in grace and giving became key in being able to accept one of the best gifts anyone has ever given me. It came from my father and it was his philosophy for life. He was a man of few words, because he believed words were powerful, so I always paid close attention to what he said. One day, I accompanied my father on one of his trips to the blood bank, and as we walked, he told me why it was important to give blood. There is power in our blood. It cannot be synthesized in a lab, and there is no substitute. Without it we die within minutes, and yet it can truly save lives.

But here is what is most important. Blood does not care what color you are or what religion you practice; how much money or how little money you have; who your parents are, or where you came from; what your fears or your dreams are. It flows like a river throughout our body. We are *all* "blood"—the term many different ethnic groups like to use as a way to connect themselves. And why shouldn't they? It's a perfect name! For blood *connects* us to each other, and my father helped me see that it represents the ultimate in giving. Giving blood is giving life, and through blood we are physically reminded of our oneness.

To find true peace in this world is to find the thread that connects us. It starts with the grace of accepting ourselves and others and accepting the circumstances of any present moment in which we find ourselves. It continues in the gratitude that we find in our own hearts and in the hearts of others. And it spins infinitely around all that we can give of ourselves and accept all that other's are willing to give back to us. We are all one in peace, beauty, and love.

Final Thoughts II

Living My Truths

~ Pilar Stella

It takes courage to grow up and turn out to be
who you really are.

~ E.E. CUMMINGS

When I embarked on this journey, I did not have a clue as to what living in the moment meant. Nor could I even possibly imagine what that would mean for changing my life once I let go of my expectations of what "it" was supposed to look like and just began to embrace what was and what came minute by minute, hour by hour, and day by day. Through the process of writing this book, I have begun to take the first steps in dreaming again about all that is possible and all that I am capable of. I have started to let go and truly dare to live my dreams.

Much of what that looks like is speaking my truth, speaking out even before I have perfected it, not holding back for fear of

219

what it might look like, and not holding any specific expectations for a related outcome. Speaking my truth hasn't always made me popular or well liked and has caused me much pain in my life, yet it has been about putting my stake in the ground and defending what I believe in no matter what the cost.

I have learned through the journey of writing this book that even just identifying the little gems of how to live in the moment has shifted me back on course to follow my true purpose, my calling, and my path. I am starting to understand that by aligning with the universe and letting things that are right come rather than chasing down the wrong things, that everything works out even better in the end. I am learning that by getting myself out of the way with my ego, expectations, goals, and plans, I am able to get back on track. When I believe in myself and trust the process, I am able to live my truths, dream *big*, and live my dreams.

I am learning that by living in the moment, I am learning to love myself and trust my intuition more and more every day. I know that all of the love and abundance that the universe has to offer will come my way and will allow me to share myself—all of myself—with the world.

I know that this simple act of giving to myself also allows me to give back even more to others. It is in this living, moment by moment, and appreciating the present, that I am able to give to others and stay connected to humanity. It is through this journey of writing this book together with Cynthia that the true gifts of my life have begun to appear and that my true purpose has become clear.

It is through the inspirations of writing this book and the journey of living my truths that *OneGiving* was created.

Share with Us in OneGiving

~ Pilar Stella and Cynthia Aliza Blake

In writing this book, we have shared with you a part of ourselves. We have embarked on a whole new project and life vision to see that each and every one of us on this planet finds ways to contribute, each in our unique ways. With this book, we hope to inspire others to find new ways to give in their life—to themselves and to others.

What are the ways that you give?

When was the first time you gave?

How do you inspire others to give?

What new ways can you find to give?

How do you give back to yourself and replenish your own soul on a regular basis?

Through *OneGiving*, it is our vision to create a community and a world of givers and giving. We aspire to learn more about the ways in which we, as humanity, give and to inspire others to give. We envision connecting givers around the world to create a global community of giving because we believe that…Together in giving we are ONE.

We invite you to send us your stories that you would like to see published in future editions of BE*ing the Present*: *101 Ways to Inspire Living and Giving*.

Visit www.beingthepresent.com and share your stories with us about how you live in the moment and how you give. We want to share your stories with the world just as we shared ours.

Visit our *OneGiving* website (www.onegiving.com) to become a part of our giving community. We hope you enjoy reading this book as much as we enjoyed writing it. We look forward to writing future editions together with you as we tell your stories!

onegiving

was created
for our
fellow travelers…
Connecting givers around the world.

Visit
www.onegiving.com.
Together in giving we are ONE!

About the Authors

ilar Stella is a powerful author and dynamic woman—full of life, passion, and vitality. She has spent her life committed to social change and giving back. Throughout her life she has walked between two worlds, between her head and heart. Yet here in this book, she has begun to strike a balance between the bi-cultural worlds of her childhood and between the "wonky" political world of social action and the centered world of living in her heart and speaking her truths. Through her writing, she is discovering her unique gifts of giving back to herself and sharing her gifts with the world. Through *OneGiving*, she has found alignment between her passions for writing, creating, and making a difference in the world.

Pilar was raised bi-culturally and grew to love and appreciate diverse cultures, languages, and people. She has traveled throughout her life and has come to recognize that despite our differences we are more similar and connected than we realize. While she is a natural extrovert, Pilar finds time to regenerate by reading, writing, traveling, taking photographs, practicing Kundalini yoga, and playing in the water.

Cynthia **Aliza Blake** is a passionate writer and life coach who inspires and empowers others to recognize their inherent gifts, radiate health, and attain success in their lives. Cynthia is committed to empowering the world through gratitude and giving. Having grown up on the fringes of society, the product of mixed cultures, her dream and vision of empowering others is truly from her heart.

Cynthia has spent her life personally living and learning the lessons of health, wellness, creativity, and success. Her extensive experiences have presented opportunities for growth and change. Her compassion and charismatic personality remain with her clients and audiences. She has journeyed into remote regions of the world, living with and sharing culture, spirituality, and native healing arts. Cynthia lives a life of purpose and passion on the island of O'ahu where she enjoys expanding her portfolio of photography and art. Her outdoor pleasures incorporate the magic and spirit of Hawaii and spending time with her husband, two of her sons, and plenty of animal children.

Acknowledgements

We would like to thank our friends and families for the gifts they have given us and continue to bestow upon us. Thank you to our WLS sisters and particularly Bonnie, Reshma, Karie, Unison, Emma, Irene, Nancy, Hillery, Melissa, and Janene who encouraged us in our journey and vision. Thanks to those who have inspired us including John, Jack, Barbara DeAngelis, Mark Victor Hansen, Gerry Robert, Ernestine, Sheli, Shirley, JC, Kathy, Earl, Todd, Dave, Byron, Zach, Zebiba, Tamara, Patricia, and David Hancock. Without your insights and inspiration, we might never have fully understood how to live in the moment while reaching for the stars and our dreams.

Thank you to everyone else who supported us and believed in us throughout the process. For your gifts and love, we hope that reading this book helps you as much as it has helped us to live in the moment. We hope that it is as much of a gift to you as it has been to ourselves.

Bonus Gift!!!

BEing the Present: 101 Ways to Inspire Living and Giving is all about being open to giving and receiving in the moment! To help you get into and keep yourself in those present moments of living and giving, we are giving you a free gift!!

We are giving you a guided meditation to help you increase your connection to giving and receiving all that you are meant to have...and give!!!

In order to help you get into the present, go to: www. beingthepresent.com and click on the *I'm Ready to Give and Receive* button.

Simply give us your name and email address and be ready to receive our email containing your gift. You will receive a powerful meditation that you can use any time!

Oh and make sure to let us know how it works for you!

BUY A SHARE OF THE FUTURE IN YOUR COMMUNITY

These certificates make great holiday, graduation and birthday gifts that can be personalized with the recipient's name. The cost of one S.H.A.R.E. or one square foot is $54.17. The personalized certificate is suitable for framing and will state the number of shares purchased and the amount of each share, as well as the recipient's name. The home that you participate in "building" will last for many years and will continue to grow in value.

Here is a sample SHARE certificate:

HABITAT FOR HUMANITY

THIS CERTIFIES THAT

YOUR NAME HERE

HAS INVESTED IN A HOME FOR A DESERVING FAMILY

1985-2005

TWENTY YEARS OF BUILDING FUTURES IN OUR COMMUNITY ONE HOME AT A TIME

1200 SQUARE FOOT HOUSE @ $65,000 = $54.17 PER SQUARE FOOT
This certificate represents a tax deductible donation. It has no cash value.

YES, I WOULD LIKE TO HELP!

I support the work that Habitat for Humanity does and I want to be part of the excitement! As a donor, I will receive periodic updates on your construction activities but, more importantly, I know my gift will help a family in our community realize the dream of homeownership. **I would like to SHARE in your efforts against substandard housing in my community!** *(Please print below)*

PLEASE SEND ME _____ SHARES at $54.17 EACH = $ $_____

In Honor Of: _____

Occasion: (Circle One)   HOLIDAY   BIRTHDAY   ANNIVERSARY

OTHER: _____

Address of Recipient: _____

Gift From: _____ *Donor Address:* _____

Donor Email: _____

I AM ENCLOSING A CHECK FOR $ $_____ PAYABLE TO HABITAT FOR HUMANITY OR PLEASE CHARGE MY VISA OR MASTERCARD *(CIRCLE ONE)*

Card Number _____ Expiration Date: _____

Name as it appears on Credit Card _____ Charge Amount $ _____

Signature _____

Billing Address _____

Telephone # Day _____ Eve _____

PLEASE NOTE: Your contribution is tax-deductible to the fullest extent allowed by law.
Habitat for Humanity • P.O. Box 1443 • Newport News, VA 23601 • 757-596-5553
www.HelpHabitatforHumanity.org

9 781600 375156